SHAPIRO'S WORLD

It's all in the FUNNIER Details

To James,

Enjoy!

Regards,

JONATHAN S. SHAPIRO

SterlingHouse Publisher, Inc. Pittsburgh, PA

SHAPIRO'S WORLD

It's all in the FUNNIER Details

SterlingHouse Books

SterlingHouse Books

ISBN-10: 1-58501-152-5

ISBN-13: 978-1-58501-152-0

Trade Paperback

First Printing–2009
Library of Congress #2009922485

Request for information should be addressed to:
SterlingHouse Publisher, Inc.
3468 Babcock Boulevard
Pittsburgh, PA 15237
info@sterlinghousepublisher.com
www.sterlinghousepublisher.com

SterlingHouse Books
is an imprint of SterlingHouse Publisher, Inc.

SterlingHouse Publisher, Inc.
is a company of the CyntoMedia Corporation

Cover Design: Brandon M. Bittner
Cover Photography: www.carynleighphotography.com
Interior Design: N. J. McBeth

Printed in the United States of America

Acknowledgements

"I would like to thank everyone that has made this possible" — words often uttered by people "shocked" to win an award, as they read from their prepared speech. I too would like to thank everyone that has made this book possible, but the reality is that there are so many who I never "formally" met and whose names I will never know, who nonetheless provided so much material for this book. For these folks, their unusual quirks, bizarre behavior and endless gifts of unintentional comedy, I will be forever indebted.

I can and would like to thank everyone at SterlingHouse who has worked so hard to bring my manuscript to life. Also, thank you to author Michael Balkind for his advice and introduction.

A very special thank you to Louis Esposito, a great friend who again and again has gone out of his way to help at every turn and has been a great confidant. Also, a big thank you (and "toast") to long-time colleague and friend Michael Rona for his extremely helpful comments on an earlier draft.

Adam Perry Lang, like a second brother for over thirty years, has provided more help getting the word out for this book than anyone else (except perhaps his wife Fleur). Rob Shapiro, my first (and only actual) brother, I thank you for decades of counsel, friendship and laughs, and for giving our family my sister-in-law Liz and their children Zach, Jordan, Rachel and Jacob. Caryn Leigh Posnansky, you are not just another sister-in-law, but also a wonderful photographer and person, and have been an invaluable help in making this project a reality.

I would be remiss (and in trouble) if I didn't thank my in-laws, Mickey and Bill Posnansky, who have always been there for my family and me and have been so supportive of everything I have ever tried. My mom Linda and dad Leonard need to be thanked for not only providing a warm and nurturing environment during my formative years, but also for providing a truly dysfunctional experience during my teenage years. Both shaped me in many ways and, as it turns out, I think the latter led me to find something funny in otherwise unpleasant situations.

To Sami and Matt, getting TiVo was surely great, but your births were clearly the best two days of my life. You have already provided me with more wonderful memories than I could ever record in this or any book.

And finally to my wonderful wife Jill, you knew what you were getting yourself into when we first met. You are a powerful woman — able to put me in my place and, even more remarkable, able to put up with me all these years. It has been a fun (and laughter-filled) ride, with many sequels to come. I love you and thank you for your support and encouragement for this and all of my projects — some more ridiculous than others.

Dedications

With love, this book is dedicated to my wife Jill and our children Sami and Matt. You each make me laugh just about every day and every day you make me think of life's wonderful (and funnier) details.

TABLE OF CONTENTS

PART THREE - Love and Marriage (and Relationships): You Can Have One Without the Others

PART FOUR - Taking Care of Business

PART FIVE - Take a Good Final Look at Yourself and the Entertaining World Around You

INTRODUCTION

While wandering through life, many are too busy or uptight to notice, or have simply become immune to, the many unusual (and much funnier) details that they routinely encounter — such as the way people behave in the men's room, in elevators or on the street when their dogs are sniffing and licking each other. Let's face it; too often many of us take ourselves way too seriously. Fortunately, the tightly wound can be loosened up and society's massive wedgie can be "picked," through analysis of the comedy that is everywhere around us.

I cannot help but recognize and analyze the strange oddities and phenomena of everyday life. In fact, even as an elementary school child I got into trouble with neighbors and teachers when I would offer them my honest assessments (borne out of my innate analytical nature), whether solicited or not, on any number of issues, including that they were dead wrong on a particular point.

Over the years, my observations of life's overlooked minutia have been met with both laughter and with questions from family and friends like, "What is wrong with you?" or "Are you under the influence of something?" My answer to the second question is usually no, while my answer to the first question is usually that they don't have the time to get into everything that is wrong with me — even though I consider myself essentially "normal."

To be sure, by many objective criteria I am a normal person (that is, to the extent one thinks any lawyer can be normal). I have no criminal record, destructive addictions or bizarre fetishes, I am married to a wonderful wife with two great kids and we live in a colonial on a quiet street in a northern suburb of New York City.

Random Aside

Everyone who mentions their spouse in a book or on an awards show says how wonderful they are. Don't get me wrong, my wife is *wonderful, but you have no reason to believe me because I would feel obligated to say that she is (which she is) even if she was a miserable bitch (which she is not).*

"Normal," of course, is a term that is both subjective and relative (especially when you hang around lawyers), but I suspect that if you decided to pick up this book, you will identify with most of the observations in the pages that follow and will hopefully find them entertaining, in which case you might be "normal" just like me! If so, congratulations!

PART ONE

Don't Feed the Humans:
Observing the Strangest Mammal of All

Chapter 1

Coffee Shop Loitering

How long is too long to hang around a coffee shop? Does the answer differ when you are using their electricity to power/charge your laptop? I am wondering this as I type these very words. I arrived at this coffee shop, which is in a large ubiquitous bookstore chain, around 9:00 A.M., and purchased some coffee and a muffin. The place is mostly empty, so it's not as if I am hoarding a table that someone might otherwise use, but two hours later I feel like it would be good form for me to order some more stuff, (especially because I just plugged in my cell phone to charge), even though I am not particularly hungry or thirsty. Then I remember that I purchased a pair of replacement headphones in the bookstore before I sat down in the coffee shop, so I prominently display the receipt on my table.

I think I will get some more coffee in a few minutes, and I think I will leave my empty cup and plate on my table so if there is a shift change, the new guy will see that I am not a freeloader who came in with his own provisions. See, I believe the coffee shop involves a type of social compact of sorts — come one, come all, plug in and tune out, but buy something every few hours and do not stay too long. Buying more stuff periodically is akin to feeding a parking meter or receiving a stay of execution — just when you thought your time was up, you get a reprieve and are now free to hang around a little longer.

One nice thing about this particular coffee shop is that, because all of the tables are really small, they are not conducive to strangers joining me to ask, "What are you working on?" Unfortunately, the chairs are uncomfortable — made of hard wood and armless and just low enough that you can't even rest your arms on your knees if you have your laptop on the table — clearly meant to discourage longer stays. Okay, I have convinced myself that this place stinks. Of course, I am not easily deterred and might stay here all day just to make a point, even if my back and shoulders are starting to hurt. I'll show them!

Random Aside

Much like chairs that discourage you from hanging around too long, it seems like some pull-out couches are specifically designed to shorten the stay of visiting friends or relatives. These "sleepers" often have a thick metal bar just below the two-inch mattress that is designed to run right across the middle of a person's back, causing considerable pain during extended stays. I've always thought these sleeper sofas should be marketed with a catchy name like "The One-Nighter," "The One-Night Stand" or "The Mother-In-Law."

I decided to purchase lunch at the coffee shop and now feel like I could stay here all night, provided that I bought a late afternoon snack and dinner. Even though this is my first time here, I feel like it has become my home away from home, despite the uncomfortable chair. During a writing break, I noticed a sign by the restrooms, stating that no unpurchased items were permitted in the restrooms and a magnetized security barrier insured enforcement of this rule. But, what if you are contemplating buying a book for bathroom reading? How would you know if it will be effective for its intended use with out giving it a little "test drive"?

Random Aside

Nothing would make me prouder than if this book were to become a staple in bathrooms everywhere — like a toilet brush or a plunger. Perhaps this book should even be sold with an optional clip that allows it to be attached to plungers? These short chapters would seem to be well-suited for trips to the bathroom. Also, hopefully this book will make you laugh, which has been scientifically proven to activate the bladder.

When I start a book, whether in the bathroom or elsewhere, even if I don't love it, I feel some type of obligation to finish it. Perhaps this is because I don't want to think of myself as a quitter or don't want the book to get the better of me. Of course, when I really enjoy a book, then I cannot put it down, it consumes my every free minute and I am sad when it ends. This is like the Murphy-Shapiro's (everyone seems to be hyphenating these days) law of book reading.

Similarly, once when I was in a furniture store looking for a real "go to" napping couch, it occurred to me that I should be able to kick my shoes off, have a cocktail or two, put some music on and settle in to see how quickly I will doze off. After all, how could I be expected to know if this couch is "The One" without giving it a road test right there in the store? Shouldn't I be allowed to cohabitate a little with the couch before agreeing to a long-term relationship? Or was this as wrong as my wife and the salespeople seemed to think?

At nearly 5:00 P.M., I finally had to leave the bookstore/coffee shop for a previously scheduled appointment. As I was leaving, I sort of felt like hugging the one guy behind the counter at the coffee shop who had been there since 9:00 A.M. when I arrived, because I felt like we had been through so much together. But then I thought better of it.

Chapter 2

"Oversharing"

Almost from birth, children are taught the importance of sharing by their parents, family members and teachers. "Sharing well with others" is one of the best compliments that can be bestowed on a child. But this is yet another instance in life where too much of a good thing can be, well, not so good.

Sometimes, "good sharers" lose the ability to properly balance their sharing tendencies when they grow up. These people want to share just about everything about their lives except maybe their bowel movements — and some would probably be more than happy to discuss those as well.

Everyone knows an "oversharer" or two and, like most personality conditions, oversharing seems to get more pronounced as a person gets older. Perhaps you are an oversharer? Or more likely, you are an oversharer in denial, as many oversharers do not recognize their oversharing ways.

Random Aside

Query whether, in writing this book, I am an oversharer in denial. But maybe by writing about my potential condition, I am not "in denial" at all. By the way, "query whether" is one of those ridiculous phrases that I have never heard outside of the legal profession. Strangely, I find that the more I make fun of these ridiculous phrases, the more likely I am to unwittingly use the very words I claim to despise — just like I did above. There was another phrase that some lawyers used at a law firm I once worked at that was intended to have the same meaning as "blah, blah, blah." I never wanted to make fun of this phrase (out loud) and even tried to ignore it whenever it was said for fear that I would start using it myself. Okay fine, if you have made it this far without turning the page, then I suppose I will share the phrase with you (but I beg you not to use it yourself) ... here it goes ... "blumpf de blumpf." I can't believe I just told you the phrase and risked its widespread dissemination. I feel ashamed and dirty now — I need a shower.

Oversharers are people who need to share every inner thought with those around them. I am a relatively friendly guy, but I don't feel compelled to share every moment of aggravation or glee in my life with complete strangers. On the other end of the spectrum are women (and I'm intentionally not being gender-neutral because oversharing does seem to be more prevalent in women) who want to share the joy that they are feeling from even the most mundane things. For example, have you ever been at a greeting card store next to a woman who must share her enjoyment of a particular card? She's smiling and nodding her head, and mouthing something like, "that's cute" or "so true" or perhaps letting out a loud guffaw, while scanning the store aisle for someone to share in this special moment. Perhaps this is harsh (but the truth often is), I don't care about strangers' thoughts and feelings on particular greeting cards. I think they should keep this information to themselves.

Random Aside

The whole idea of pre-printed greeting cards makes no sense to me. Apparently you care just enough to send someone a card, but not enough to take the time to write a personal message? (I suggest going with a blank card and writing something other than your name or not sending one at all.) Then there is the never-ending campaign to convince people that they need to get everyone they know a card for every occasion — like the "Congratulations on Your Move to a Larger Cubicle" card or the "Sorry to Hear You Have Herpes" card. I am apparently "supposed" to get not only my wife (my "Valentine") a card on Valentine's Day, but also one for every woman I know — including my mom, aunt, secretary and the lady that always helps me at the post office. At least the card store makes it easy for the consumer by having a special "Valentine's Day Cards for the Lady at the Post Office" section, as well as other random categories, all with pre-printed cards that include appropriate greetings so you don't need to come up with anything original for the lady in the Post Office.

Some people "overshare" their pets, wrongly assuming that strangers want them to climb all over them. On a warm summer evening in Manhattan a few years ago I was waiting to pick up a prescription in a drug store and otherwise minding my own business. A middle-aged customer arrived at the pharmacy area with a large, mangy dog that looked like it had not been cleaned or combed out in months. The dog owner was hugging her "little baby" and saying things like "Oh yes, pretty girl!" Although I like dogs, I'm not a big fan of dirty, stinky ones, and as this dirty, stinky one headed my way sniffing and slobbering, I made it very clear that I was not interested in playing by leaning away. My clear sign of disinterest was, of course, ignored by the oversharing owner, who, probably believing that everyone must love her dirty, stinky mutt as much as she does, allowed the dog to get "into my personal space," so to speak.

I tried in vain to move away, but I was trapped against a display case and the dog proceeded to give me an enormous, slobbering, lick from my ankle all the way up my leg to just above my knee. ("Luckily" I was wearing shorts.) When I reflexively winced and said "Awh, nasty," Miss Dog Owner, apparently perplexed that I wasn't thrilled with my saliva present, asked with disdain: "Oh, are you allergic or something?" Of course, being in a no-win situation, I did what usually gets me in the most trouble with women like her: I told the truth, stating that, "I'm not allergic ... but, um, actually ... I just don't like to be licked by strange dogs." She then shot me the "what a jerk" look and pulled her stinkasaurus away as if to shield it from the mean "animal hater."

Many parents suffer from a Postpartum Oversharing Problem (also known as "PoOP"). These folks think their kid is the cutest ever born and is the apple not only of their eyes, but of all their friends and even of complete strangers. Of course, most babies (of all species) are very cute, at least early on — this is evolution's way to encourage care for the young, I suppose. Anyway, parents suffering from PoOP can often be seen looking around feverishly for the slightest sign of approval from strangers in response to any movement or sound produced by their "genius" and "beautiful" child.

Random Aside

I recognize that this is a shameless and sophomoric effort to use the word "poop." As discussed at length in Chapter 4, however, I believe "poop" jokes are always funny — from the cradle to the grave. Even the mere mention of the word "poop" can be funny. If you are not convinced, stand in front of a mirror and say "poop" six times, in ascending levels of volume, followed up by four quick, loud "poopies." If you don't find that funny, someone overhearing you certainly will. In any event, and most importantly, the thought of anyone actually trying this has made me laugh.

At a loud diner or at a playground, for example, most child behavior is acceptable and may even be entertaining. But some parents battling PoOP inexplicably think that they should share their child's squeals, whether of joy or pain, with strangers in quiet, adult settings. Of course, it makes no sense to voluntarily bring a young child to a setting such as a quiet restaurant, where acting his or her age would be a problem. Context is key, a simple notion that is routinely lost on severe PoOP sufferers.

One of the worst cases of PoOP that I ever witnessed was at a wedding for one of my wife's former colleagues. The parents of two toddlers let their children run back and forth (over and over again) in the back of an old church whose floors creaked with every step, much to the delight of the kids, who laughed and giggled and shouted tortured pronunciations of their first words. Under different circumstances, this behavior could have been entertaining, but these kids carried on (as you would expect kids of their age to do) so loudly, and for so long (perhaps for thirty or forty minutes), that it was very hard to hear much of the ceremony. While many people turned around on numerous occasions to stare-down the cute little noisemakers and their mom, each time, the mom, filled with apparent joy — and PoOP — would smile with an expression that said, "Aren't they just precious!"

I was getting enraged just on principle (or perhaps because I kept nodding off and the kids were waking me) that Ms. PoOP did not take her kids outside, but I was not really in a position to say anything because I could not have been more tangentially involved in this wedding. I had never met the groom and had only seen the bride a few times. I was shocked that no one closer to the action (just about anyone else) didn't explain to the mom that this particular event, a wedding, was, surprise, surprise, actually supposed to focus on the couple getting married and not on her kids. Amazingly, some lose all their common sense when they have kids. For them, I offer a few simple tips: Most people, particularly strangers, don't want to hear your kids singing or screaming in an otherwise quiet, serious or official setting. And, just because your child has the cutest little sneeze doesn't mean that strangers want him sneezing on them!

Similarly, many PoOP moms (I have never known a father who did this) write notes as if they are *from* their one-year old child. I suppose this is an effort to "share" the child's unspoken (and, of course, really cute) thoughts. Don't get me wrong, it's great when a kid is able to scribble a picture or a message or much of anything for that matter. Until that magical day, however, these moms must be told that notes "from" their infant saying things like: "Thank you for coming over to play with me. I love my new truck!

Let's have another playdate soon!" are really annoying (unless their one-year old actually wrote the note, which would be very impressive). Perhaps no one has had the heart (or lack thereof) to mention this before, but I specialize in dolling out tough love.

To be sure, it is not just young mothers who are guilty of over-sharing. As these moms get older they are likely to be oversharing recidivists — about their (then grown) babies or grandchildren. The cell phone is often the weapon of choice for these and many other oversharers. I am sure you have witnessed women in their 60s who must let anyone within earshot (on a commuter train for example) know that they have an amazing "new" invention called a cell phone. "Hi Shirley, I'm calling you from the train on my CELL PHONE! Heh, heh ...." As they scream into their new-fangled communication device, they scan the train car for an approving glance.

Because some people are so loud and obnoxious when using their cell phones, it has caused a strange backlash against even normal cell phone usage. Many find it okay to be considerably louder than everyone else when speaking to someone next to them, but that same loud talker then will glare menacingly at someone speaking in low conversational tones on a cell phone. They might roll their eyes and swivel their head in a "Good Lord!" fashion, as if the person were shooting up heroin or drowning a puppy. Perhaps they are just upset that someone is not paying attention to their loud conversation?

Other people (mostly men) are notorious cell phone oversharers when discussing a big purchase, big bonus or big promotion at work. It's usually necessary for these guys to include some big numbers in their loud chat so people within earshot can fully appreciate the magnitude of their Mr. Big Money status. I have also noticed that when a cell phone rings on a train or in another public place, five or six people (again, mostly men) quickly reach to check if it's their phone that's ringing, even if the ringing is clearly coming from a different direction. I suppose it's possible that these folks are trying to be considerate by quickly checking if it's their phone that's ringing, but I suspect that most, at least subconsciously, reach for their phone to announce to any who notices that they are very important and that any minute they are likely to receive an important call.

Men overshare in other ways, as well. One middle-aged, heavy set guy in the vestibule of my commuter train exhibited a unique oversharing/show-off move as the train pulled into Grand Central Station. He adjusted his hair, tucked in his shirt and then re-positioned a pamphlet that was sticking out of his shirt pocket so that the words "My [New York] Giants Account" were clearly visible to all. This pamphlet, flaunting to any and all that he is one of the fortunate few Giants season ticket holders (there's a waiting list about forty years long), was used like a clothing accessory — like an expensive watch, meant to announce that he is "big time."

My brother told me a story of another oversharing-on-a-train award winner. One morning, he and a few friends entered their train's vestibule to find a guy who — once the area was filled with people — proceeded to chug a full liter bottle of water. Apparently he was very proud of his chugging abilities. (Sounds strange, but I have a friend that is similarly proud of this type of liquid in-take prowess, although this friend of mine is himself a little strange). When the Chugger finished the last drop of his water, he was greeted with some mock clapping and he then said, excitedly (to what he apparently understood as his adoring fans): "Did you notice that I didn't even take a breath!"

Random Aside

Bumper Stickers are really a form of oversharing. Why the need to tell complete strangers how you feel on random issues? "Member of the Clergy who loves porn!" T-Shirts or buttons are often "human bumper stickers." I particularly enjoy the clothes that proudly advertises the fact that the wearer is really annoying — like t-shirts trumpeting that the wearer is a "Drama Queen" or the "World's Biggest Bitch." How about the shirts that simply warn "Stay Away!"? The irony is that the people who wear such "warning signs" are not likely to get mobbed by groupies or get mistaken for supermodels.

Some people on my commuter train ride to Manhattan cannot sit quietly for any period of time and must seek out complete strangers with whom to chat. There's at least a 50/50 chance that one particular such guy is clinically insane (he has a madman's grin and shifty eyes) and whose train ride could be part of a limited amount of time that he has each week "on the outside" (in between shock therapy). This way-too-friendly guy always sits down in train seats that face each other and smiles while trying to involve himself in other people's conversations, even if the person across from him is talking on a cell phone. It's nice to be friendly, but please, at least, once in a while, read a book or newspaper, sleep or write a ridiculous book (like this one). Do something to fill the time without prying into the lives of every stranger who sits next to you. I find my iPod acts as an excellent oversharing defense mechanism, much like how garlic wards off vampires. Not only does it drown out the loud yapping between passengers, but it also protects me from being sucked into a conversation with a random madman, or just a well-meaning oversharer.

Random Aside

Unfortunately, some people overshare something far worse than conversation on the train, namely their odors. Some overshare bad breath or that awful "I just could not get around to showering this morning" smell, while others overshare tuna fish platters or other stinky food that is clearly not suitable for unventilated areas.

Another important oversharing defense on commuter trains involves seat selection. I always try to sit on the aisle of a three-seater and hope that no one wants to squeeze between me and the guy by the window. And if I have the option, I will always go for the row with the really large guy sitting by the window who is spilling over on to the middle seat, figuring that nobody in their right mind would want to sit in that middle seat. But this strategy is not without its risks. If someone not in their right mind decides to squeeze into the middle seat, they will likely spill over on to me and I will be forced to crank my iPod extra loud and hang over my arm rest into the aisle like a droopy plant.

One of the many bizarre things I notice during my commute is how often seemingly able-bodied people will choose to squeeze between two very large, sometimes snoring, people, rather than stand. Standing just seems like a much more attractive option. But that's just me. When a train is crowded, I have on occasion taken a seat in the (dreaded) grouped seats — which face each other, yet have so little room between them that if all seats are inexplicably used in the group, folks are forced to alternate their knees and place one in the crotch of the person facing them or contort themselves in some other manner to avoid grinding with a stranger. If you are familiar with these awfully configured seats, then you know that the four-seater can only comfortably hold two people and the six-seater three (alternating directions), unless there are children or love interests involved. I'm amazed when someone tries to squeeze in (as the third or fourth in a four-seater or as the fourth, fifth or even sixth in a six-seater) and, essentially, "spoon" with a stranger for the ride. These are over-sharers, of sorts, essentially looking to share an intimate moment with their fellow passengers.

Speaking of intimate moments, on the Tuesday before Christmas, 2008, I boarded my train heading to Manhattan, with designs on editing this very chapter. The train was definitely emptier than normal, with many already taking off for the holidays, so I decided to "risk all" and take an aisle seat of a completely empty four-seater. The only upside of the grouped seats is that there is more room for a laptop, as there is no seatback, from a seat in front of me, just off my knees. A few stops later, with many empty seats still available throughout the train car, a middle-aged, able-bodied woman approached and placed some bags by the window seat diagonally across from me. I shifted my body to allow her access to this seat so we would both have room and be relatively comfortable. Instead, she (amazingly) proceeded to sit in the seat directly across from me. Our knees banged as she strategically positioned her feet in and around mine (recall, these facing seats simply cannot fit two adults). At that point, I thought (or perhaps hoped) that she was just a "train rookie" and needed some helpful guidance, so I poked my head out from behind my laptop and nicely suggested that, "It might work better if you slide over," as I motioned to the window seat next to her.

"Oh no, I like the aisle," she replied matter-of-factly, "but if *you* want to slide over..." motioning to the seat next to me! I did a partial eye roll and just put my head back behind my laptop, without saying a word or taking my headphones out of my ears and ignored her as she droned on a bit more. Of course, I immediately started to record this incident and as I typed I thought about moving over to the seat next to me where I would have been much more comfortable. I never moved —opting again for discomfort on principle. Boy did I show her! She was much shorter than I am and seemed pretty comfortable. She even stretched her legs straight under my chair, as I typed away (about her) and uncomfortably shifted my body towards the aisle.

Random Aside

It may seem hard to believe that this incident happened while I was editing this chapter about oversharers, including train oversharers, but as the clichés say, "Truth is stranger than fiction." And, "You can't make this stuff up." Regarding the cliché, is it possible that the word "cliché" has become cliché? Interestingly, it seems that this very question has, itself, become cliché, as a search of "cliché" on Wikipedia makes this same "clichéd" point.

Now, if you think I was angry about my unsolicited train encounter, you would be wrong, I was not. It has taken me decades to realize that oversharers who still do not understand basic rules of human interaction are not sources of aggravation, but rather are sources of entertainment ... and material for my readers to (hopefully) enjoy. As discussed above, the roots of oversharing stem from preschool lessons about the virtue of sharing with others. Similarly, didn't everyone learn by the time they were five-years-old that the first person on a bus, an amusement park ride, the classroom rug during show-and-tell, or wherever, gets to choose their seat? Did I mention that I was the first person to take what should be the only occupied aisle seat in an awkwardly configured four-seater? I was first! Shouldn't this have ended the issue? In Kindergarten, it would have.

Chapter 3

Elevator Rides and Other Awkward Moments

Small talk about the weather (for example, "Nice weather we're having, huh?" or "Well, we need the rain.") must be the most popular conversation filler during awkward moments of silence. Weather filler like, "Gonna be a hot one!" is often heard on elevator rides among co-workers who don't know (or want to know) each other too well. They might as well say, "I have absolutely nothing in the world to say to you. In fact, I have more to say to my neighbor's cocker spaniel than I do to you and, quite frankly, I can't wait for this elevator to reach my floor so I can get away from you."

Random Aside

Remarkably, there are some people that do not find silence in the presence of others awkward at all. These people are happy to sit next to you on a long drive or at a ballgame in complete silence for long, long stretches of time. I am not one of these people, so when I am with one of them, I often feel the need to say something every 10-20 minutes, if only to confirm that they are alive. Two lawyers with whom I used to work (both great guys by the way) are such "comfortable silent types," that when I heard that they attended a Yankee game together, I was eager to find out how it went. Apparently they had a great time, although sure enough when I pressed one of them, he conceded that neither made so much as a peep between the second and fifth innings of the game.

An elevator is one of the great forums for awkward moments because strangers are trapped together in a very confined space. Some elevator passengers stare quietly ahead at the changing floor numbers, anxiously awaiting their stop and trying not to make eye contact with anyone. Others (oversharers) prefer speaking loudly while looking around for an approving reaction from fellow riders. A really annoying elevator rider is the stranger who interjects him or herself into your conversation ("Oh, yeah, 'Fletch' was a great movie.") or answers a question that you and your friend are pondering, usually as he or she is leaving the elevator and with a smart-ass, satisfied look ("Oh, by the way ... the capital of West Virginia is Charleston"). I have also seen men (no, not me) suck in their guts and talk about their (alleged) recent workout to try to impress attractive women passengers, many of whom then leave the elevator rolling their eyes.

While waiting for a bus in Manhattan, I witnessed an awkward situation akin to an elevator ride, when two men, complete strangers, were unwittingly brought within a few feet of each other as the dogs they were walking stopped to greet each other. These men were like people stuck in the elevator — waiting to be released from each other's presence. The dogs sniffed each other and licked each other's genitals. Needless to say (and fortunately), the dog owners did not get as intimately acquainted. In fact, they didn't say anything to or even make eye contact with each other. They simply held their leashes and looked the other way (much the way people in an elevator stare at floor numbers), and after five minutes of public canine fornication, they gave each other an uncomfortable nod and slinked away — like strangers that wake up next to each other hung-over and wondering what happened the prior night.

In general, the male greeting, unless among close friends, is often awkward and definitely not very touchy feely. It usually consists of two parts, the first being a "Hey," "What's doin'?," "How's it goin'?" or "How are you?," and the second part being "buddy," "guy," "man," "chief," "dude" or "sport." This superficial hello doesn't require learning or recall of anyone's name. And often after this "warm" greeting, neither party has anything else to say, except maybe a generic comment about "last night's game" or, like on an elevator, some weather filler.

Growing up on Long Island, I noticed a female version of this, usually during Christmas or Thanksgiving break from college at a club called Sprats. Girls would run into each other and they would (while giving each other fake air kisses) say something like "How ARE you!?" "How's Syracuse?!" (pronounced SAAH - RAH - Cuse); "How's Maryland ?!" (pronounced MAH-RAH-Lind); or "GW?!" (pronounced GE -DOUBLE-Yooouu). "Do you luuve it?! Luuve it?!" Then they would move on to the next person, because they really had nothing to say in the first place. These superficial male and female greetings are really not much different than the dogs that sniff each other "around back" and then move on to the next dog or hydrant or tree.

The "kiss hello" (whether a fake air kiss or not) can also create some very awkward moments. When is the appropriate time to transition from the handshake to the "kiss hello" with an acquaintance or friend? This switch can be very tricky, particularly when one person might believe a kiss is warranted and the other a handshake. We've all been there ... you move in for a kiss, the person puts out their hand and you try to play it off like you always intended to shake. It can also be awkward when you have a personal relationship with someone who you encounter in a business setting. The handshake seems odd, but in this context, in the presence of co-workers who may not know of the pre-existing relationship, the "kiss hello" appears bizarre and makes everyone in the room look at each other wondering "What the heck was that!?"

The "kiss hello" can also be made awkward when greeting a group of people in a social setting who you know to varying degrees. Kiss, kiss, shake, kiss. Sometimes, perhaps to avoid "leaving out" or "depriving" someone of a kiss when you are kissing the other members of the group, you end up kissing a person who you barely know and then feel weird about the whole thing. Then, the next time you see them, you have to try to break the kiss cycle with a handshake and act like the kiss never happened. Years ago at a charity event I ran into a former colleague with whom I never really had much of a relationship. Even though she was not among a group of people who I knew to varying degrees (as discussed above), somehow, in a moment of temporary insanity (perhaps trying to be cordial, but going way overboard), I gave her a "kiss hello" in a situation that clearly called for a handshake at best. I will never live this moment down, as friends who were there still joke about this.

Finally, yet another danger from the "kiss hello" is inadvertent lip contact. This occurs when you try to give someone a kiss on the cheek and at that very moment you and the person both turn heads, causing a sloppy, wet kiss to accidentally get planted on the lips. This scenario is particularly uncomfortable when you are 14 and you kiss your friend's mom.

Like the "kiss hello," conversations with complete strangers on the telephone can sometimes be awkward despite the relative anonymity. Am I the only one who has ever felt the need to disguise my voice, for example, when calling back a restaurant reservationist with whom I just spoke moments earlier? Also, am I the only one who thinks that when people ask the question "Am I the only one?", they are confessing to something strange and simply hoping there is someone out there as strange as they are, or at least someone who might admit to engaging in the same behavior, to reassure themselves that there is nothing wrong with them? When I was younger, I felt really uncomfortable after I'd make a reservation and then realize that I needed to call the restaurant back for some reason (e.g., address, dress code, etc.). At this point, I (like others, I'm sure) would try to disguise my voice to avoid hearing the reservationist say "Didn't I just speak to you?" Sadly, Caller ID foiled my voice disguise plan years ago.

The advent of Caller ID has led to some awkward moments. When I notice I have a missed call on my cell phone, I will often call back the number displayed. Sometimes a person who misdials me denies that they made the call, even though their number is on my cell phone. I usually cannot let it go. "No, I think you really did call." Just admit to misdialing and I will let you go on your way! Somewhat related, and equally annoying, is when someone calls me on the phone and then within moments decides that it is not a good time for them to have a phone conversation. It's as if I placed the call to them and interrupted an important business meeting. My usual (smartass) response is to say: "Did you call me at a bad time? I'm really sorry that I inconvenienced you by answering your call." Then there are the people who call you on your office or home number and ask: "Where are you?" Ahh, hello?!

Which reminds me, how did the word "hello" come to mean both "hi" as well as "what the @#$!?" Are there other words in the English language with such drastically different meanings? It would be as if the word "family" also meant, when said with a certain inflection: "I want to beat you with a stick." I suppose that when stuck in an elevator or waiting for your dog to stop licking a stranger's dog (or the stranger), words like "cold front" or "big storm coming," might as well mean "When will I be paroled from this personal hell!"

Chapter 4

Hitting the Men's Room

At this point you might be questioning my claim that I am essentially "normal." Like it or not, however, I am normal and an adult, at least by most objective criteria. In fact, as a husband, a father of two, a homeowner and a lawyer (with no criminal record), one might even suggest that I'm a responsible adult.

Random Aside

The word "adult" can have many different connotations, depending on the context. An "adult" home or retirement community is obviously very different from an "adult" film, which probably has nothing to do with "adult" education or the type of "adult" who must accompany someone under seventeen to an R-rated movie. The same word, pronounced the same way, can mean over the age of eighteen, over twenty-one (i.e., post-college-aged),

> *over sixty-five or just over-exposed and*
> *over-sexed.*

Nevertheless, amusing crap about goings on in the bathroom (bad pun intended), or scatological humor as it's known by its more "adult" term, is always entertaining. If I'm in a public bathroom and someone really lets one rip (called a "crackle" in our house), it's very difficult not to laugh. In fact, I often must bite my lip to keep from laughing. And forget about holding back laughter if I'm in the men's room with one of my friends or with my brother — we might as well be little kids again. I think most people, if honest, would admit that these moments are as funny today as when they were preschoolers. Remarkable really. What other type of humor is so universal from cradle to grave? Sadly, our final years in this circle of life can once again feature crapping ourselves and diapers. Perhaps this is a cruel way to punish us for laughing at poop jokes our entire lives.

Some people — the "scatological humor proof" — appear to be so serious and/or well-read that they like to think that they are above this sophomoric stuff. But even these folks can inadvertently let their guard down, if only for an instant, allowing their instinctive/primitive side to take over. One ill/well-timed crackle can even make mourners laugh or bite straight through their lips to avoid laughing.

Scatological humor appears to be instinctively amusing. I remember a clip on a nature program of a chimpanzee sitting on a branch laughing as he peed on the head of a chimp on the ground. When my son was around two-years-old he would start laughing hysterically, whenever he would let one loose. Of course, I would try to explain in a serious, adult tone that while this is a normal bodily function, well-behaved people try not to do it in public. All the while, my son would laugh and wait for me to join in, with an expression that said, "Come on, old man, you know this stuff is funny, so stop holding back a laugh!" When he was five, he kept a running "crackle tally" for more than a week. We were watching a movie and he shifted his body, giggled and said, "62nd time crackling." A few days later, while I was reading to him in his bed and he was just about asleep, he whispered, "102nd crackle."

There is a cute children's book called "Everybody Poops" that teaches kids that it is a natural thing done by all people and animals alike. Still, most people don't announce when passing their company's receptionist on the way to the bathroom to "please hold their calls because they had burritos last night and it's gonna be awhile!" Yet, if you pass the receptionist while heading to the men's room with a newspaper under your arm, you are, essentially announcing "POOP TIME!"

You may be an executive in an expensive suit, meeting with board members concerning the future direction of the company, yet right next door lurks the primitive world of the men's room, which might as well be a cave lit by torches. There, on a break from weighty corporate issues you will be hard-pressed not to laugh if someone really let's one rip or if you hear a guy in the stall "fighting the good fight" and making grunting sounds like he is giving birth. Maybe it is precisely because the business of life can be so serious at times that men's room business becomes such a universal form of comic relief.

Random Aside

I think it is literally possible to die laughing. When I really crack up, I make very little noise, start tearing and wheezing and can barely breathe. This happened the first time I saw the bathroom scene in the movie "Dumb and Dumber" (your classic "spike the guy's drink with laxatives and sit back and watch the fun begin" scene). I was laughing so hard my wife thought I was having a heart attack. I was on all fours

> *gasping for a breath. To this day, when someone mentions that movie, my wife says that it almost killed her husband. I experienced a similar scare a few years earlier while attending a George Carlin stand-up routine during college.*

The whole concept of the shared public bathroom is strange. Think about the private (and far from odor-free) moments experienced only a few inches from a complete stranger in the next stall, separated only by a one-inch think stall door. Yikes! Given these circumstances, you would think *everyone* would try their hardest to seize upon whatever minimal opportunities for privacy exist. Not so. Some people living and working among us inexplicably choose a middle stall or urinal in a triple stall/urinal "formation" bathroom. I cannot comprehend why anyone would willingly choose to "ride shotgun" to another guy emptying his bowels and/or bladder. This is simply poor bathroom etiquette. I'm sure even cavemen spread out a little further from each other when they did their bathroom business — wild animals do. And please, when using the urinal, remember to stare straight ahead. Looking down to either side at your neighbor's stream and saying "Hey Jim, lookin' good!" is generally not well-taken.

Some men apparently have the need to show the world that they can pee "hands free" (or "wireless"). It's like the " X Games" for the bathroom — the "extreme urination" event. I have had urinal "neighbors" who prominently fold their hands up high by their chest or loudly slap both hands on the wall above their urinal, as if they were getting frisked by the bathroom attendant. I have also (unfortunately) seen people checking out their nails or loudly yawning while stretching their hands up in the air. I have never been able to fully understand the message these men are trying to convey. Are they impressed with their ability to go "hands free," like some type of bicycle trick ("Look Ma, no hands!")? Perhaps they think "hands free" relieves them of the need to wash their hands? They would be wrong, of course. Also, just in case you were wondering, washing hands — with soap after conducting any bathroom business — is not optional! And by washing, I don't mean simply waving one's hands over the sink or through the water. The "faucet wave" will not wash off the fecal matter, urine and other germs contained in this cesspool of contamination, and does *not* count!

Some small men's rooms in restaurants have a truly odd set-up: One urinal and one stall-less toilet, with a lock on the door. Are these bathrooms built for one or two? They seem to be "conflicted singles," much like a guy who is not sure whether to get engaged to or break up with his girlfriend. I supposed one interpretation could be that if you just need to use the urinal or wash your hands, you are expected not to lock the door, but if you use the toilet, you definitely should lock the door and enjoy that moment all to yourself. Perhaps the better rule is to simply lock the door under all circumstances. Of course, this is often the only men's room in the restaurant and if it was meant to be for only one person, why the urinal? To discourage sloppy guys from peeing on the toilet seat, I guess?

If you are using the urinal or the sink (for washing of course, you sicko) in one of these "conflicted singles" bathrooms and you don't lock the door, when someone enters, he will probably think he has walked in on you. Then you have to explain that you don't think it's a single bathroom and he'll have very little room to stand as he waits for you to finish — a very awkward situation for both parties. It would be a good hidden camera gag to capture the reaction of people who walk in on a guy (in on the gag) sitting on the toilet in one of these bathrooms (remember, no stall!) and reading the paper as comfortably as if he were at home. The man entering would be embarrassed, but the toilet guy would say "No worries, it's not a single bathroom, help yourself to what you need." And then, while the man is washing his hands, the toilet guy would make all sorts of foul, straining noises or ask the gentleman at the sink to pass him some tissues or toilet paper, or to answer his ringing cell phone in his jacket that is hung up on the back of the bathroom door.

The cell phone — the newest appendage in human evolution (Darwin would be proud) — has created some interesting bathroom etiquette issues. Non-stop cell phone availability adds to the exaggerated importance that most people place on their business affairs. Remember before cell phones, when doctors got paged, sometimes for life and death medical emergencies? Most cell phone users don't spend their days saving lives or solving problems like world hunger, but their need to be available (at even the most private of moments, like in the bathroom) makes it seem as though their affairs are similarly important to mankind.

Random Aside

The human race survived for thousands of years without cell phones. But then the cell phone was invented, we broke down and bought ones with thirty minute per month plans "for emergencies" — like when my wife was pregnant with our first child. Fast forward a few years and now everyone has a cell phone (called a "mobile" if you are European, or American and want to come off as worldly and well-read). Many of these people believe they and everyone else should be accessible via cell phone during every minute of every day, even though there are (thankfully) so few real emergencies in life.

Sometimes a person, like say ("hypothetically") your father-in-law ("hypothetically" named Bill), can get very upset when he leaves multiple non-

emergency messages on your and your wife's cell phones and you do not get the messages for an hour or two — even if you spoke to him just moments before his first message and he knew you were going to a dinner with friends — because even though it was not an emergency, "it could have been one!" Your "hypothetical" (and wonderful) father-in-law could then leave a series of messages, the last of which features him screaming that he has "a GREAT IDEA ... you and your wife should take out your cell phones, throw them on the ground and SMASH THEM to pieces, because they are useless! No one can get in touch with you if there is AN EMERGENCY!"

Some folks take cell phone calls in public bathrooms. I can't comprehend this. There is the whole issue of handling the phone and your privates (and the transfer of disgusting stuff from one to the other) and where to put the phone when you need to use both hands for your bathroom business. Also, who really wants to be on the other end of a conversation with a guy struggling in a bathroom stall?

Random Aside

I refuse to use any type of belt clip for a cell phone or PDA, even if it might make some sense. If you can, God bless I cannot. At one time I had four different "devices;" Batman's utility belt would have been the most efficient thing to hold all of them. I also refuse to use a man-purse, or "murse," or "European Carry-All," which is essentially a

> *women's handbag masquerading as a leather toiletry case. Whatever you're into, that's fine with me. I find that sometimes a blazer works nicely as a sort of murse surrogate, with many additional pockets to hold all of my items (I'm down to two devices and, as always, a wallet and keys), and is preferable to the other options. But that's just me. Like much of this book, however, this is all besides the point, assuming there is a point here or anywhere else.*

If your cell phone rings when you are in the bathroom, I have a crazy suggestion ... let the call go to voicemail! Is this so complicated? Are you so important that the world can't wait for you to complete your bathroom visit? Please!

Needless to say, I have experienced this scenario first hand. I was washing my hands (thoroughly, I might add) at the sink of a bathroom in my office building when a cell phone sitting on the sink started ringing. Apparently the phone belonged to a guy at the urinal who I had seen around and only knew well enough to exchange hellos in the hallway. He looked over to me and smiled. Feeling awkward (and wondering what my responsibilities in that situation were), I said something like, "They really don't leave you alone, do they?" The guy laughed and I started to leave, but as I was doing so, I wondered if, even only for a moment, he might have actually expected me to answer his phone and walk it over to him at the urinal. Of course, "it goes without saying" (yet many of us feel compelled to say it anyway) that I would never have done this, but I was wondering what he was thinking. If he was expecting a really important call, might he have said, "Hey buddy, could you just answer that and tell them to hang on one second?" or "Could you just pass that thing to me?" Presumably, he could have tried to interrupt his pee in mid-stream and answer the phone himself, but this is very difficult and definitely not advised.

Bathroom and bathroom-type odors present other concerns. "Masking agents" to cover up these odors are often not much better that the odor themselves. Many bathrooms these days, in addition to being equipped with automatic flushers and faucets, also have automatic motion sensor air fresheners. I find myself moving stealthily around the men's room (like a jewel thief trying to avoid the electronic eyes protecting the Hope Diamond) to avoid being repeatedly pelted with the "mountain fresh spray."

Stinking up the bathroom is one thing (that is, after all, where society has decided the stink belongs), but stinking up the "outside world" is a whole different story. "Crackling" in an empty elevator before getting off is like setting a land mine — the next person enters in horror and is stuck in the cloud of stench. When additional people then enter the elevator, the first guy that walked into "it" begins making disavowals like "wow ... some guy before me...." Similarly, if you are in your private office at work and a "crackle" happens to sneak out just as a co-worker (usually of the opposite sex) appears at your office door to ask you a question, the only thing to do is to quickly jump to your feet and meet the co-worker at the doorway and suggest to "discuss this issue in the privacy of the hallway...." This, of course, has never happened to me!

In the men's room, people routinely blame the "mystery man" who stunk up the joint before them, but perhaps in these situations we must remember the elementary school proverb: "Whoever denied it, supplied it!"

Chapter 5

It's All About the Attitude

"Attitude" is everywhere, to varying degrees. For instance, it appears that the amount of attitude one is likely to get from a store's salesperson is directly proportional to the store's prices. There is a significant difference between the amiable sales staff at The Gap, as compared to staff at a really expensive clothing store on Fifth Avenue. Is the extra attitude something that is worked into the price? Are we actually paying extra for the humiliation? Often these salespeople, who (like most folks) cannot themselves afford to regularly shop at the store, act as if they own it and look down on customers who cannot afford a more expensive item? "Well ... we do have some more 'economical' items in the back if you want to rummage through the sale rack...."

A few years ago at a "fine" men's clothing store, I was looking at their "slim-fit" dress shirts (even though I was a few pounds heavier at the time), which as the name suggests, are cut smaller around the gut. A saleswoman approached me and asked, with a raised-eye and a cross-examination style tone, "Have *you* ... worn these before?" Clearly a euphemism for "don't you think you are too fat to wear this cut?"

Sometimes, teller window attitude can be pretty severe as these people behind the glass tightly control that little light that says "They are now *finally* ready to serve you." Whether they are a bank teller or working one of the windows at a train station ticket counter, I have seen some of them rule their little empire with an iron fist. I witnessed a woman make the unforgivable mistake of approaching an Amtrak teller's window just after a customer was walking away but before the little light was turned back on. Before the woman reached the window, the annoyed teller pointed up to the un-lit little light and said: "Uh, uh, please wait for the light!" The exasperated woman (in line for at least the 20 minutes that I had been there) dropped her head and started walking back to the line. Moments later, the teller put on his light letting the customer and everyone else know who was in charge and that now he was ready to serve.

Random Aside

Years ago when attending a charity auction in Manhattan, I noticed auction attitude. Perhaps you have too. When there is heavy bidding for an item at least one bidder acts like James Bond bidding on a Picasso, while continuing to raise the stakes. Mr. Big Money taunts and teases his opponents and the crowd as he waits for the caller to count (while, looking in Big Money's direction), "Going once, going twice, ... going three times," and just before the gavel comes down, while looking around the room Mr. Big Money slowly raises his paddle, while smirking and bobbing his head up and down. Oh the drama! Just like Mr. Big Money likes it. In the end, he is the

> *proud owner of a very unremarkable item. He then usually exchanges smiling pleasantries with his table and the crowd, before taking a big deliberate sip of his drink — as his head moves quickly back and then forward, along with his drink — this is an "attitude swig." If you have not noticed this before, you will now. The "attitude swig" is sometimes followed by the "attitude chew," which involves exaggerated, open-mouth gum chewing and is often accompanied by a winking of one eye.*

Some people have "positions of power," while others need only make slight changes to their wardrobe to ratchet up the attitude. When some women put a hat on their head they develop an instant attitude — something I refer to as "Hattitude." This is usually first displayed by college-age girls wearing a baseball cap, sometimes backwards or sideways or a cowboy hat at a bar. Fifteen or twenty years later they are wearing a wide-brim hat and strutting their stuff — feel the power!

Then there is restaurant-related attitude. Sometimes I get attitude for simply asking a waitress a second time for something that was not provided, despite clearly including it in my order. I always ask nicely (the first and second time), recognizing that the waitress has a hard job and anyone can forget something. And that is why it is particularly intriguing when I get an eye roll and the "what a jerk" look. (If they knew me better, this might make sense). This has happened on many occasions — most often in Japanese restaurants, with requests for tea or low sodium soy sauce (perhaps you just rolled your eyes, although the doctor says I need to watch my sodium intake — are you happy with yourself now!). While I can't speak Japanese, I do find it curious that some waitresses in Japanese restaurants in Manhattan don't seem to know English words like "tea" and "check." I would think that these words would be among the very first one would learn in this setting, along with "water," "tip," "bathroom for customers only," "police" and all curse words.

The most attitude I have ever experienced, however, was at one of the old-school steak houses in Manhattan in the mid-1990s, which is still subject to my personal ban. My wife and I had reservations (did I mention that we had reservations) on a Saturday night with two other couples. First, they made us wait almost an hour in a bar area that was as packed as a subway car during rush hour. Of course, there was no big apology for the delay; no "can we buy you a drink at the bar for your inconvenience." Oh, no. Part of the problem was that I did not realize that the restaurant was doing me such a favor by serving me and my friends and taking our money. If I had fully understood this, I probably would not have gone in with the expectation of being treated like even a semi-valued customer.

Eventually we were seated at a cramped table in a cramped dining room and when the obnoxious waiter took our order the fun really began. Now, I happen to like my steak only a little pink in the middle — not "black and blue" and not with a red and/or cold center. I usually order my steak medium or medium well depending on the restaurant's description of how they cook their meat. Most great steak places, like Del Frisco's, are more than happy to accommodate and sometimes suggest that they "butterfly" the filet — slice it down the middle and spread it out so they can cook the center more — and it comes out perfectly.

Strangely, some very insecure men think that "real men" do not get steak this way. I don't understand how the rareness of steak correlates to manliness, except perhaps on the theory that it is somehow more akin to chasing down, killing and devouring your prey — i.e., ripping apart raw meat with your teeth — in the wild? Nonetheless, this seems like an issue for jerks like this waiter. It would seem, in any event, that if this is how I want my steak they would accommodate, but not Mr. Big Shot who knew much better than I how I really should want my steak. When I ordered my steak medium well, he laughed and said, "You're kidding, you don't really want it that way — I don't even know if the chef would do that." I responded in kind telling him that I knew how I like my steak and that it would be appreciated if he would just put the order in like I asked. (I am sure I got an extra helping of spit on my steak, because again "I'm the jerk").

A few years ago at another steak house in Manhattan, I was having a wonderful dinner with friends, we had drinks, a few bottles of wine, many, many courses, dessert, coffee, after dinner drinks — the point is that we were spending a lot of money. Just as we are enjoying the last sips of expensive Port, the Maitre-de came over to our table and gave us a warm smile and a hello and asked how everything was and whether he could buy us a round of drinks.... At this point, I was thinking, now this is the way to treat good customers and perhaps this could become part of our regular steak restaurant rotation (it was our first time trying this place). Then, the Maitre-de added three little words to his otherwise nice welcome and offer of drinks — he said he wanted to buy us drinks "at the bar." He is kicking us out of our table!? It is not as if we were chatting for thirty minutes after coffee. Perhaps if another party is waiting for the table, he should buy them a drink at the bar — after all we are sitting. We were all probably done drinking, but decided to take him up on his offer and ordered a round of their most expensive Port (I think it was $40.00 a glass) at the bar and the restaurant never became part of our regular rotation.

Attitude is served (usually cold) at much less expensive establishments, as well. In diners I often get attitude from waiters when I ask for skim milk (doctor says I need to watch my cholesterol) and they bring me whole milk instead. I try to be nice and ask for the skim milk again and often they bring it over without a fuss, but sometimes the guy will give me major attitude and claim that what he has delivered to my table is, in fact, skim milk. If you have ever seen the two liquids you know that they look very different, but sometimes the waiter will be insistent. This starts to piss me off. On one occasion, after some back and forth regarding whether it was skim or not, I conceded (for the purposes of argument) that perhaps it was two percent milk, but I was sure it was not skim. The waiter held firm and said that it was not two percent, but rather skim milk that he poured out of the carton himself and I am pretty sure he called me a jerk under his breath as he walked away in a huff.

At that point, I was actually finding the whole affair more humorous than anything else, but I was still sure that I had not been served skim milk — and, of course, could not let it go. When a waitress passed by I asked her for skim milk and Ms. Honest and Polite indicated that the establishment did not have skim milk, but she could offer me two percent milk instead. (Is a little honesty too much to ask for?) While having my "ah-hah" moment and feeling vindicated, I looked across the room and noticed my original waiter glaring at me like he wanted to take our skim milk disagreement outside. Have people fought to the death for less? I am not sure, but am still pretty convinced that I could take that punk.

Chapter 6

↓ Put on a Happy Façade ↑

Often when smiling Maitre-des or wait staff ask "How is everything?" or "Is everything all right?," it is clear that they are not actually expecting a response other than "Fine, thanks." They ask these questions, often even before you have been served anything but bread and water, while moving past the table, as if it is merely a greeting, such as, "Hey, how you doing?" They are not expecting you to list everything (or any of the things) that are not going so well. It is like when saying to (not really asking) a Jewish grandmother, "How are you?" Some may think this is just another way to say hello and may be taken aback when she responds: "How am I? How should I be, my hip hurts, my ankle hurts, I can barely see or hear ... I wish I was dead."

"Okay, great, speak to you soon, love you grandma!" While grandma is telling you exactly how she feels (about everything), some restaurant employees hide their true feelings about the situation and instead offer a smiling façade that they hope will appear believable. To be sure, if everyone just played along, it certainly would make things easier for these people.

To varying degrees, and depending upon the circumstances, many will temper their true feelings about a particular subject or situation and try to "keep up appearances" — if the situation or those around them does not get the better of them. For instance, some men try to project an always sunny façade. These are the guys with the perma-smile (like a game show host) and the "hey, how ya doing, everything is wonderful and how can I help make your day more special" way about them. These guys can sometimes be found in New York, but are rarely originally from New York and try to project a Midwestern charm. Judging only from the surface of this constant smiling façade, many people would inaccurately describe these guys as "warm and nice and truly concerned about others."

The dead giveaway with this type of façade is that no one can be as happy or nice as the Midwestern Charm Guy claims to be, all the time. I much prefer people who are more genuine and easier to read, even if that means an occasional mood swing. The guy who just seems too happy and smiley all the time, often has a very dark scheming side. (This is also the kind of guy who may have a secret love interest with a farm animal behind the back of his wonderful family.) I have dealt with some lawyers like this (not certain about the farm animal part) and they repeatedly display the smiling happy game show host bit, until you catch them doing something really sleazy (which these guys always seem to be really good at). Then, when called on the sleazy maneuver and, I suppose now pushed just enough, Mr. Midwestern Charm will lose his cool and go absolutely ballistic. I recall this happening once and I must admit it was rather delightful when the façade was destroyed and the guy's true colors shined through. With a big smile, I calmly responded to the now Red-Faced Irate Guy: "No need to get so excited, Chip."

Sometimes the façade is used to hide one's true interest or motivations concerning a particular activity — to keep up appearances that whatever they are doing is not that important. Some parents at youth sporting events may not be screaming like lunatics, but if we were able to hear their internal monologue (or perhaps track their stress level) we would know that deep down some really do care — a lot. In these situations, many parents don't want to demonstrate how competitive they are and just how important it is to them that their six year-old daughter's soccer team wins its "big" game.

Random Aside

A strange but related phenomenon involves the façade as a defense mechanism to protect very competitive people in the event they do not live up to the expectations set by themselves or others. I think this is the explanation for why some people run the New York City Marathon dressed in a chicken suit or some other head-to-toe costume. (No joke, many, many people do this every year). Running the marathon is tough enough without adding a heavy and uncomfortable costume to the mix. If you have ever seen these costume-clad runners, many are moving very fast and seem to be very accomplished marathoners. Yet, for some, I suspect putting on the costume allows them to project to others (and convince themselves) that they are not really taking the race seriously. Just think how good their time would be if they wore shorts and a tank-top, stopped all of the clucking noises and chicken dancing, and really tried hard?

I have witnessed another example of the chicken suit phenomenon at a bowling alley. My friend Garry (not a typo, he

> *spells it this way) and I took our kids to bowl and near the end of our game, a family started bowling in the next lane. No one was bowling with a costume on, but we noticed that the late 30s early 40s mother in the next lane, a lefty, was bowling with her pocketbook secured over her right shoulder and her right hand tucked in the right front pocket of her jeans. Garry and I were intrigued by the "bag lady." She and her pocketbook bowled with the carefree "I don't really care about my performance" attitude for the first six frames before Garry and I, reluctantly, had to leave the bowling alley and this interesting show. Of course, the amazing part was that she had four strikes and a spare among her first six frames! We had to leave so we do not know what her final score was, but think how good it might have been had she put down the pocketbook and used her personalized ball, bowling glove and specially designed rosin bag.*

Another façade of "mild interest/competitiveness" can be seen when people fight like dogs for a table at an outdoor public space such as Bryant Park, in Midtown Manhattan, but display a warm, patient disposition. When the weather is nice on a spring or summer weekday, hundreds and hundreds of people pick up lunch and bring it to these large outdoor spaces. Friends spread out and try (aggressively, but without looking that way) to find an empty table or more likely wait for an empty table to open up. One strategy calls for hovering near those who seem to be done or near done with their lunch, although there is an attempt to seem as if the hoverer is not rushing the diner. The hoverer's façade says:

"Take your time, all day if you need to, no worry." Of course, one sign that the table may be opening up — a wipe of the mouth with a napkin, a last sip of soda, some evidence of table cleaning or even feet shuffling — and the hoverers move in and move in fast. If you shift in your chair and appear as if you may be getting up (think: the old television game show "To Tell the Truth") — people who seemed to be just relaxing nearby, will quickly scoot into position and move in for the kill.

Another strategy (my preferred) is to walk briskly (but, by no means, run) from one end of the park to the other and the instant someone starts getting up you continue (at the same measured pace) towards the table. If you are not moving toward and almost approaching these tables within one to two seconds you have no chance, as the entire table "turnover" process during peak times is a two to four second event. (I have timed this).

For a successful table acquisition one must go at it without even a moment's hesitation and without catching the eye of another pursuer. If you do not make eye contact with the competition — even if you did not see the table first — they will 99 times out of 100 let you have the table, if you get to it first. This is somewhat analogous to when drivers act as if they do not see a driver in the next lane who is trying to get their attention and merge in front of them. Most drivers who manage to avoid such eye contact feel that they do not need to allow the would-be merger to pass. One must move quickly for a table, for sure, but an all-out sprint is clearly poor etiquette and is frowned upon.

Once my brother and I were walking past some tables on the way out of Bryant Park, when we noticed a table open up and two young women, who were together, briskly walking towards the table. At the same time, another young woman, with her head down, was sprinting towards the target. The two competing factions seemed to arrive at the table at the same time and the sprinter acted surprised to see the other women when she looked up from her dash. They both looked at each other — neither party seemed to be immediately giving up, yet I was not sure if they knew how to resolve this situation on their own.

At this point, the Good Samaritan (or wise ass) in me took over. While I am only a few feet past these women and while still walking, I called out — motioning to the two women (the non-sprinters) "it's their table." It definitely seemed to me like the parties needed a ruling and I was more than happy to adjudicate the dispute and help keep the peace. In case you were wondering, I stand by my ruling — the sprinter broke the unwritten rules of engagement for lunch table takeovers or perhaps this should be described as "behavior inconsistent with custom and usage in this area." In any event, as my brother and I walked away we had a good laugh over the fact that the sprinter quickly conceded the table and totally accepted the "ruling" of a passerby.

PART TWO

The Media and Popular Culture: Did They Screw Us Up or Did We Screw Them Up?

Chapter 7

Local News Banter

Weather reports on the local news seem to go on and on, yet do most people really care about the barometric pressure, the dew point or the record temperature on a particular date? Then they break for commercials before the five-day forecast. Please, just tell me if it's going to rain today and if I'll need a jacket — of course, this could be done in under thirty seconds.

Then there is the banter between the aptly titled "weather man" and the other anchors. I love how they act as if he actually controls the weather — like Bob the weather man is the all-powerful Weather God or perhaps Mother (or Father?) Nature himself. Every night the over-animated local news anchors, including the men wearing way too much make-up, turn excitedly to the Weather God and say something like "Bob, please, please tell us you have good news for the weekend."

If the weather man "gives" them good weekend weather, they praise the almighty Bob: "Yeah, Bob!" "We love you Bob, you're the best ... thanks for bringing us that warm front for the weekend." Yet, the anchors can turn quickly on Bob if he gives them a bad forecast: "What!? You've *got* to be kidding ... rain this weekend!? ... Bob you need to work on that forecast!" Also, there is no accountability for a wrong forecast. When it turns out to be a beautiful day, despite the prior day's forecast for heavy rain, the all-knowing weather deity never admits to blowing it. Instead, he usually mumbles something about a cold or warm front and "getting lucky" and "as we thought might happen" (but never told the viewers) "the storm pushed off to sea before reaching the area." When the weather guy gets it wrong, but we are treated to great weather, it is like receiving a gift for no occasion (the "just because" gift). In this case, "just because" the weather guy loves you, the viewer. The day after the weather guy predicts nice weather, but misses the typhoon that blows into town, is usually when you hear "sitting in for Weatherman Bob is ...."

When I was attending Fordham Law School at Lincoln Center, I would often see the local news weathermen who worked at stations nearby and wondered if they always carried an umbrella with them — even when they thought there would be no rain. Think about this scene: They miss the forecast and are on line with everyone else in the rain trying to buy a five dollar umbrella from the local newsstand. Wet viewers would be shaking their heads in disgust and muttering things like, "Ohhh ... Mr. Weatherman, no rain today, huh?!"

The prominence of the weather forecast in the local news is really part of a larger issue, which is that the "news" so rarely reports news. Many would differ on the definition of "news" or "newsworthy," and on some level if people continue to watch and presumably care about what is being "reported" on the news, then by definition it is newsworthy. But please. The amount of time devoted to coverage of crime, accidents and fires — essentially "bad" or "scary" news — or "news" about celebrities is astounding, especially when compared to the time devoted to such things as politics or issues impacting war and peace, the environment, or economic, social or health issues. Sure, you could argue that the local news covers politics when they report on the Mayor of a small town getting caught sleeping with his children's babysitter and that the story about the crack addict who gets stabbed in an alley is really about economics and health concerns, but sadly it is the scary and messy affairs of the day or absolutely anything about celebrities that many people want to see. And, as is obvious, the local news (much like most free television) is selling advertising space and is giving the people what they want, but it is still sad that so many people watching consider themselves "informed" about the important issues of the day.

Random Aside

It would be nice if the news was more honestly re-titled something like "Crime and Scandal Today." At least with shows like "When Animals Attack, Part 37," you know what you are getting and can tune in with the family if that is your idea of good family entertainment. Also, it would be refreshing if, when the networks interrupt their regularly scheduled program with what they call a "News Alert" — but which frequently is not news at all and will even more frequently not necessitate an alert — they would make clear that they are interrupting in order to scare the crap out of the viewers and encourage them to watch more so-called news.

The News Alerts come fast and furious when there is some snow in the forecast. Television news people must love snow — the continual warnings and teasers for news programming that will provide us, the viewers, with "the latest" on the potential snow "dumping" that will likely be "of biblical proportions." And then they repeatedly cut live to our favorite weatherman. He is usually dressed down before the big news show at the top of the hour — he's working so hard for us that apparently he had to take off his jacket and tie and "roll up his sleeves" — and is in some type of Doppler weather bunker imploring you to tune into his most recent, accurate forecast of the potentially "historic" storm during the next hour. To be sure, if it is expected to be a really big storm (as with any really big "news" event), they will come up with some catchy title, like "Winter Blast [insert year]" or "Massive Dumping of Snow that Might Kill You, So Stay Tuned!"

A favorite feature of the local news is the "live" shot. This often involves a reporter standing in front of a non-descript brick building where, in a room inside and completely out of view, and earlier in the day or yesterday, something allegedly happened. There is absolutely nothing to see behind the live reporter on the scene, but oh boy is it gripping! Another award winning "live" shot is when they send some poor schlep out in a blizzard or hurricane so you can fully appreciate the magnitude of the "weather event" in the area. There is nothing better than watching the reporter hang on to a tree for dear life as he or she warns viewers not to go out in the dangerous conditions unless it is absolutely necessary — like to get a "live" shot.

The "chopper-cam" is still another favorite, especially when they go live before they have any idea what is going on. Sometimes it goes like this: A news anchor, off camera, says, "We are apparently viewing a high speed chase," and then after some confusion and shots of the anchors playing with their earpieces, the anchor, again off camera, explains what is actually going on in the live shot: "Um, apparently, um... our reliable sources are now telling us that the driver in the late-model Toyota that we have been watching and the State Troopers that we thought were in pursuit are simply both getting Big Gulps at 7-11." Then they cut back to the studio and a concerned looking anchor says something like: "Wow, that was a close one, thank God no one got hurt" and the co-anchor delivers an agreeing “Amen!” — at this point they both look shaken as the station cuts to a commercial break.

If you think the local news anchor’s job is easy, you are crazy. They have to display more emotional range than most Oscar-winning actors. The transition from the “genuine concern for humans and puppies face” (when reporting on a tragic story), to the “happy cheery face” (for the very next story about a celebrity wedding), is just awesome. It usually takes two “happy” stories (i.e., four minutes) after reporting on a really horrible tragedy before the anchors are again ready to yuck it up with the weather guy — assuming the forecast looks good.

Chapter 8

Who are "They"?

Sometimes you will see people in an absolutely horrendous outfit that is not the least bit flattering, but they will emphatically and enthusiastically proclaim that this is what "they" are wearing or what "they" are showing? Well who is/are "they?" Where do "they" come from? What do "they" look like? Do "they" have monthly meetings — like the Board of Directors of They? Where they sit around and decide what everyone else will wear and or what others should say?

The nameless/faceless internet is a form of "they." People proudly proclaim that they (not to be confused with "they") read something "on-line" or saw something on some website concerning something of importance — like an emerging fashion trend or a life-saving treatment, as if merely mentioning that they saw something on their computer screen makes it a reliable and verifiable source.

Random Aside

Similarly, who is Lazy Susan or her fast cousin "Saucy Susan?" Who is "Pete," you know from "for Pete's Sake" and is he related to Peat Moss? And who is this "Well Enough" guy that older people are always concerned about and imploring to "just leave alone?"

If while reading this random aside, you (1) thought to yourself "wow, this guy is an idiot" and/or (2) pondered what the real "answers" to any of these questions were, then you need to (a) stop taking every moment of life or yourself so seriously; (b) have a drink or three or take some valium or other prescribed medication; or more likely (c) consider some combination of (a) and (b).

Speaking of what "they" are wearing, apparently Silver is and has always been the "Official Color of the Future." In virtually every movie depicting the future — the people are always wearing silver-colored outfits. I guess in the future "they" will say that "silver" is the color to wear? With hindsight (or I would argue even without) many fashion trends are absolutely ridiculous. Look at the gym shorts that NBA players (and society in general) have worn over the last few decades — from the one extreme of the tiny tight "short shorts" (much like the Speedo "marble bag") to the other extreme of huge baggy shorts which cover from halfway down a guy's butt to the middle of his calf. Neither of these choices made or make any sense; they neither look good, nor are they comfortable.

Random Aside

In terms of more appropriate men's swimwear — shorts-like suits — often the only discernable difference between them and a pair of shorts that you might wear at the gym, is that the former has a "garage." Because one does not wear anything underneath a bathing suit (unless one is a complete freak or not potty trained), most men's suits have a convenient netting (or "garage") that allows neat storage of the all-important equipment in the water. One of the true joys of fatherhood was explaining the "garage" concept to my son when he was five.

The way kids wear pants that are suspended in some manner across the middle of their butt is, if nothing else, bizarre. They have to constantly adjust them so that they are low enough, but do not completely fall down to their ankles. Have you ever seen a kid running for a bus with these Halfway-Down-Your-Ass Pants? They run with one hand hanging on the back of their pants as if they are running to the toilet and might not make it in time. But apparently this is what "they" say young people should wear. I suppose we should be thankful that "they" apparently do not say that balding, overweight forty year-old accountants should wear their pants this way.

Obviously people in the fashion industry have a financial interest to encourage people to buy the latest thing, but often "they" are not in the fashion business. Instead, "they" may be a small niche of clothing wearers who start a fashion fad, for example some kids or rappers or movie stars attempting to do something different, which ironically causes many others who want to be "different" to do the same as everyone else. The bottom-line for me on what "they" say to wear is that there is often no rhyme or reason to what is selected as the new thing. A fairly recent phenomenon was that "they" decided that it was not totally inappropriate and sloppy to wear a dress shirt untucked hanging out over jeans in non-work settings. This one I like because, although random, it is actually much more comfortable than having the shirt tucked in your jeans.

Random Aside

Long after I first wrote this chapter, I heard of an apparent "fashion idea" (probably now "so last year") called the "Pee Wee Herman" look, involving men's clothing that was too short and tight! This is about as random as it gets, but does, I suppose, make those who have put on a few pounds, appear to be "stylish." The first time I really gained any weight, as an adult, I thought that either my pants (then riding a little higher) had shrunk or that I was experiencing a really late growth spurt. It turns out that one needs longer (and eventually wider) pants as the weight gets packed on. I guess that was the something new that I learned that day!

I am half expecting one of "them" to decide that next year the cool thing to do is to roll your left pant leg up over your knee and say something like "Yeah dude, we're going left up." Sound ridiculous? Perhaps, but "left up" would seem to be as random as some of the other things that "they" are doing.

Chapter 9

Am I a Superhero?

It is times like when your car is out of gas, in the middle of nowhere, when many wish they could simply blink and transport themselves to their comfortable bed or perhaps a tropical island. From an early age many people wish that they had superpowers. Perhaps they wish they could fly, turn invisible, had healing powers or the ability to instantly transport themselves from one location to another or back and forth in time. It all sounds good to me, but unfortunately I was not born with gifts that would have given me instant membership in the SuperFriends' Justice League of America. When I was a kid I watched the "SuperFriends" cartoon, but never understood why the likes of Superman and Wonder Woman, who had really cool superpowers and could save the planet by themselves, needed or put up with the "Wonder Twins" with their rather random powers.

In case you don't remember this show, the female "wonder" twin (Jayna) could turn herself into different animals — often a bird that would carry her brother (Zan) who would transform himself into a water or ice formation. Also, there was a ridiculous blue space monkey named "Gleek." What did he add to the SuperFriends' planet saving work? They might as well have had Gilligan hanging around "to help." Speaking of random super-powers, why not have a SuperFriend that can reduce/enlarge himself — like a 3D copy machine — perhaps he is normally a 6' 200 lb. man, but can reduce himself to 3' 50 lbs. or enlarge himself to 9' 400 lbs. Perhaps he could be called Adjustable Man? I have to assume this power could come in handy, at least as much as the Random Twins and the damn monkey! I liked the show anyway, especially the deep-voiced narrator that would say, "Later, at The Hall of Justice!," seemingly every five minutes.

When I was in college I finally gained a greater appreciation of random powers when I discovered that I too have a random superpower, of sorts, although to date I have been unable to properly harness it to save the world, my family or even a few bucks. My "power" is the power of facial recognition. While many people claim they "never forget a face," I really never do and will demonstrate below the extent of my "powers" in this area. Medically speaking, I might be said to have the opposite of a disorder known as "prosopagnosia" or "face blindness." People who suffer from "prosopagnosia," cannot distinguish one face from another, except for those who are the most familiar to them. The condition is thought to be the result of a defect in a single gene or to be caused by a brain injury — which makes me wonder if my "condition" has been enhanced by many shots to the head. My "powers" have been joked about extensively over the years with my friends and my wife, although in the end they have all come to understand (and at times marvel) at my facial recognition prowess.

Random Aside

I think it took years to realize that I had this gift because without many, many years on this Earth I did not have an opportunity to use or express my powers. In other words, I needed to see many, many new faces and see some that I had not seen for years and years to fully understand, test and display my special ability. For example, if every item on Earth weighed no more than twenty pounds, how would Superman, or anyone else on Earth, fully appreciate how strong he was on our planet? Did you follow that analogy?

Now, you may be very skeptical at this point and with good reason. It is hard to believe that someone possesses superpowers, even when the alleged powers are rather random ones. Perhaps you can be convinced.

If I meet someone once, many years later I will recognize them. I recently saw a guy entering a restaurant and realized that he was the criminal court judge (out of context, with no black robe) that presided over a two day trial in which I was a juror about ten years earlier. Not impressed yet? Do not worry you will be. I see people all the time that I recognize from my days as a bartender during college in the early 1990s — people that I really did not know, but who I served a few times. Also, on almost a daily basis, I notice people on the streets of New York or in a restaurant or store who are actors or actresses, news anchors or professional athletes — even if they are without any makeup, totally dressed down or wearing, for example, a hat and dark sunglasses.

One of the interesting "wrinkles," if you will, regarding my powers is that I am able to "age" people. In other words, I will see someone, say in a restaurant, and will realize that they look just like I would imagine someone that I once knew (even if only barely) would look like today — even if I have not seen the person since they were teenagers or nursery school. In fact, this happened on two occasions a few years ago within a month of each other in restaurants on Long Island and in Westchester. On each occasion I saw a woman that went to my high school (one a year behind me and one two years ahead of me); one was an acquaintance, while the other I did not know at all and I had not seen either of them for at least twenty years. Are you impressed by my powers yet?

In the Spring of 2000, my wife and I went to brunch with a friend and her new boyfriend at the time, who we had supposedly never met before. After exchanging pleasantries, I said that our friend's boyfriend looked very familiar to me. My wife, of course, rolled her eyes (this was before she developed a true — present day — appreciation for the extent of my powers) and said something to the effect of "sorry my husband thinks he knows everyone." It seemed that the boyfriend and I had never crossed paths — different professions, grew up in different areas, different colleges and professional schools and he was about nine years older than me, as well. Could my facial recognition powers be letting me down? I was sure there must be some connection, but my wife was relieved when I finally dropped the inquiry.

Of course, this continued to bother me for days, as I wondered where I had seen this guy before. See, my "gift" is often more of a curse because if I recognize someone and do not instantly recall where I know them from or their name (which I rarely do recall), I then endlessly rack my brain until I figure it out or am able to finally put it out of my mind.

Random Aside

There was a time when I would approach people that I recognized as someone that I once crossed paths with ten, twenty or thirty years ago and often they would not remember me or claim not to remember me or think I was a crazy stalker. In any event, for the overwhelming majority of these sightings — of people with whom I never really had any relationship — I would have absolutely nothing to say after confirming my suspicions that we did, in fact, cross paths (perhaps it was the kid who moved away in second grade or was on my brother's little league baseball team or whatever). I stopped approaching these people because I realized all I was doing was confirming my powers to myself. During his early days on Earth, didn't Superman pick up random heavy objects for no apparent reason, except to prove that he could, until he too became secure and comfortable with his powers.

A few weeks after the brunch, my wife and I got together with the same couple and randomly the boyfriend mentioned a sleep away camp in Pennsylvania that I spent two summers at when I was ten and eleven. "Ah, hah!" I exclaimed. The riddle was solved. It turned out that twenty years earlier the boyfriend was a counselor (when he had a full head of hair and no glasses and was about nineteen-years-old) one year when I was a ten year-old camper. We figured out that our bunks were a few doors down from each other and I would have certainly seen him from time to time during what was his last and my first year at this camp.

I felt relieved because I would no longer torture myself trying to figure out where I knew this guy from. More importantly, however, my facial recognition powers, which had been called into question, were proven to be worthy of a place among the SuperFriends — well maybe instead of the silly monkey. Also, this was a defining moment in that after this incident (and to this day) my wife does not doubt my superhero powers, at least in this one area!

Chapter 10

Where is the Remote?

My childhood was plagued by a very dark time in television history, a time before cable TV when there were very few viewing options. Only a few channels existed and there wasn't 24-hour programming. Late at night, channels would switch to a test pattern and an annoying beeping noise or an American flag and the National Anthem. Reception, such as it was, was courtesy of rabbit ear antennas. "Kids" out there reading this must be wondering how we "old folks" survived (much like how my generation wonders how our ancestors survived without electricity and indoor plumbing) and how I turned out so normal. But wait, my tale of woe gets worse.

There were no remote controls! If you are under twenty-five, read that sentence again. That's right, you had to actually get off your butt to change the channel. Oh, the horror! Many lazy people suffered through some really bad television and the show "lineup" — a channel's shows on a particular night — seemed to really matter. Some really bad situation comedies heavily featured the laugh track, which may well be the all-time worst television "innovation." I refuse to watch any show that has a laugh track. Why watch a show so un-funny that there is a need to be reminded (by hearing recorded laughter), that what was just heard was considered funny by the show's writers? Congress should do something about this.

The absence of competition and remotes back in the day, probably explain why some shows were so bad, yet lasted as long as they did. "Mr. Ed," which seemingly ran for an eternity, was about a talking horse! "The Munsters." Need I say more? There was simply nothing else on! How do you think Mr. Ed would have fared against successful shows of the last few decades like "Seinfeld" or "CSI"? My guess is that viewers would hit their remote controls faster than Mr. Ed could say: "I don't want to be glue!"

Random Aside

"CSI," a great show, reminds me of "Quincy M.E.," a show that aired from the late 1970s until the early 1980s. Quincy starred Jack Klugman as a Medical Examiner who was outraged every episode about some injustice that he was hell bent to correct. A great and often overlooked part of the show was Quincy's status as a lady's man, highlighted in the show's opening montage. Quincy looks like he is examining a cadaver, but then the camera pans back and we see that the body he has his hands on is a very much alive, young woman in a bikini on the S.S. Quincy! With no disrespect intended, Jack Klugman would not have been among People Magazine's "Most Beautiful People," had such a list existed back then. Nonetheless, at the time, I don't think viewers felt that Quincy's

> *sexual prowess was a stretch. After all, this was around the same time that viewers were buying into the idea that Fonzie had mystical powers over the ladies on "Happy Days." In retrospect, Quincy's "popularity" with young attractive women was much more believable because at least he, unlike Fonzie, was a gainfully employed, educated professional who made a positive contribution to society.*

Given the slim pickings on TV when I was growing up, I would frequently watch "Gilligan's Island." Like most viewers of "Gilligan's Island," certain things puzzled me, such as why the Castaways were able to fashion a communications satellite out of coconuts and chewing gum wrappers, but they couldn't fix a damn hole in a boat? Meanwhile, were we really supposed to believe that, stranded on that island, nobody had sexual relations with the lovely MaryAnn or Ginger? Heck, after a few days on that island, Lovey Howell — even the Skipper — would start to look good! Also, why would people going on a three-hour boat tour pack *any* luggage, let alone multiple outfit changes? Ginger had countless glamorous evening gowns, even though it is not clear why she would have worn even one gown on a boat tour. Incredibly, though, the Skipper and Gilligan — who ran the three hour tour (and maybe even lived on the boat) — seemed to only have one set of clothes!

And did you ever see the one where the Professor came up with an elaborate contraption — made, of course, with nothing but coconuts and seaweed — to signal for help or transport everyone off the Island, only to have everything screwed up by Gilligan? Perhaps step one of any escape plan should have been to kill Gilligan. How hard could that have been? By the way, is it possible that the Professor on "Gilligan's Island" was related to MacGyver?

Do you remember the show "McGyver?" He would be handcuffed and locked in a safe at the bottom of the Atlantic Ocean, yet with only a match, some string and belly-button lint he was easily able to escape before the commercial break. What an American hero!

Just as an unsuccessful rescue off of Gilligan's Island was always a "surprising" twist, so too was it always "surprising" that every episode of "Scooby Doo" ended with the revelation that "Mr. Johnson!" was disguising himself as a ghost to try and scare away Scooby and his pals from some hidden treasure. And, of course, the scheme always "would have worked if it hadn't been for those meddling kids!" My son was excited the first time he learned that "Scooby Doo" was on television when I was a kid and that I regularly watched the show. When he asked about my favorite episode, I asked him if he had ever seen the one where Scooby and the gang were scared away from some treasure by a ghost that turned out to be Mr. [fill in the blank]. Matt, five at the time, knowingly nodded his head and said, "Yeah ... that sounds familiar."

As cable television took off in the 1980s, competition from additional channel offerings and the need to fill programming slots resulted in many new shows and even some improved quality. But cable also meant that we would still be treated to reruns of "Gilligan's Island," "The Brady Bunch" and other average to poor shows from the past. The advent of cable also led to the explosion of what is often the best comedy (albeit unintentional) on television — the infomercial.

The host is always so excited about the miracle product! The audience is always shocked and amazed by the miracle product! Then there is the guy on the show — the "Dupe" — who does not realize the amazing powers of the bag in which frozen meat cooks to perfection in ten minutes in the microwave. He starts to do things the "old and difficult way." The Dupe says things like, "Well, Jim (Mr. Host), I would normally take the frozen block of meat out of the freezer and defrost it for six days in the sink or in the hot sun."

Such comments always make the Host really, really excited. Mr. Host, with a big, toothy smile and a wink, shakes his head and says to the audience members' delight, "not anymore you don't!," and proceeds to demonstrate the miracle of the moment. The audience members, who had been on the edge of their seats waiting for the miracle demonstration, are once again very satisfied and happy. The Dupe is always a bit confused, as it takes him a little longer to fully comprehend how the miracle product has changed and perhaps even saved his life, but he eventually comes around.

When it comes to unintentional comedy, however, the infomercials are still a distant second to some actual radio and television advertisements that cause me to wonder, even if for only a moment, whether they are real or some SNL-type spoof. I recently heard a radio ad where two women are discussing a new convenient health care provider that turns out to be associated with a New York City-area pharmacy chain wherein, as one of the women excitedly explained "you can get your blood drawn." I highly doubt that having any medical procedure performed at this pharmacy, even just blood work, ever occurred to even a few of this pharmacy's many customers. No doubt, these pharmacies are everywhere, at least in Manhattan, where you can usually find one within a block of every Starbucks, so I suppose getting lab work done there could be convenient from a location standpoint. But so would getting medical treatment at a McDonalds. I assume the pharmacy has a separate, private sterile area where trained medical professionals take blood, but I can't erase from my mind the many downtrodden, miserable, former DMV employees I have encountered at these stores who, upon checking their weekly shift schedules, would learn that they are needed to cover an under-staffed "blood" shift later in the week. I further picture a miserable cashier simultaneously calling for a price check and asking if anyone is free to take a customer's blood in the condom aisle.

I heard another radio favorite when I was in Florida visiting my mom a few years ago. Within minutes of getting in our rental car at the West Palm Beach airport, we heard the following radio jingle: "DOC-tor SHA-pi-RO, Hair IN-sti-tute!," followed by a young, inquisitive girl asking, "Dad, how come you have more hair on your back, than on your head?," and closing with the catchy jingle "DOC-tor SHA-pi-RO, Hair IN-sti-tute!" Is it really necessary to make a joke here? And can there possibly be a better market for Dr. Shapiro's services than in the Boca Raton, Boynton Beach and West Palm area? There must be more bald men and comb-overs per square mile there than in any other place on the planet. Also, with medical science now permitting many of these men to "perform" as if they were decades younger, it stands to reason that they would want to fill in their bald spots, as well. And by the way, take it from a Shapiro (although, no relation to the good doctor in question), it is no small feat to come up with a jingle for "Dr. Shapiro Hair Institute." Pretty impressive stuff.

In my opinion, the winner for the greatest unintentional comedy in the "real" ad division goes to the commercials for the electronically-adjustable beds. Has anyone ever looked more uncomfortable than the people in the featured "comparison" flat beds from hell do? They squeeze two large, old people (who probably have had both of their hips replaced) into a toddler-size bed made of wood and give them each one tiny straw pillow. Then we the viewers (or at least I) sit back and laugh as these folks toss and turn, then toss and turn some more, all the while grimacing and rubbing their lower back pain.

While (some) improved television programming was certainly a welcome development in my life, it was nothing quite like the truly life-changing experience provided by two small packages that I received (approximately two years apart) many years ago. Although, it may seem like I am referring to the births of my two children — which certainly were the best two days of my life and the greatest gifts I have ever received — I am actually referring here to receipt of my two TiVo DVR's. Once you truly experience TiVo's wonders and splendors (and to a lesser degree the "other guys" DVRs) it is like you are part of a TiVo-cult and it is your duty to share your love for this innovation with anyone about whom you care. And I care deeply about anyone who purchased this book. (If you borrowed this book, or stole it, well, let's just say that I don't care about you quite as much.)

Television today has many, many viewing options, but still very few quality programs. TiVo allows me watch the few shows, and many sporting events, that I actually want to see, when I want to see them and, by skipping all of the commercials or breaks in the sports action, in less time than if I watched the shows live or started the games on time!

In a strange way, TiVo is/was like a fountain of youth, seemingly making my remaining days on Earth longer, or at least more efficient! I have always thought that TiVo's sales slogan should be "Live TV is for Suckers!" Even if I happen to be available at 8:00 P.M. on a Thursday night to watch an hour-long show that airs then, there is no reason for me to start watching at 8:00. (Why would I want to be a sucker?) Instead, I can do something around the house or enjoy doing nothing at all, perhaps take a nap, whatever, between 8:00 and 8:15, then watch my show, skip through the commercials and still finish at 9:00 P.M. — the same time that those who have not yet converted to TiVo (or some inferior DVR product) finish watching. Also, if you have to go to the bathroom or get a drink or break up a fight between your kids, you can simply pause the action — whenever you want, not when a commercial break allows — and not miss a thing! Did I mention that I love TiVo?

Random Aside

While you may be wondering if my unbridled enthusiasm (and love) for TiVo is some sort of product placement-type deal I've entered into, rest assured that it is not (at this time). I truly love TiVo and have from the very first moment we met (I can remember the details), but I am not being paid to say so on these pages. Of course, I would be more than happy if TiVo wanted to send me some money for spreading the TiVo gospel to those who have not yet found this religion.

TiVo's ability to pause live action, rewind it when I have not quite heard something or want to see something again and skip through boring stuff is phenomenal. Unfortunately, it doesn't work in my non-television viewing life. I have been at live sporting events and found myself trying to pause the game or rewind it, my thumb involuntarily pressing down as if the (glorious) TiVo remote were in my hand. When my kids are attacking each other, I want to pause them, rewind to figure out who started it or fast forward to the part when they are getting along really well again and learn hopefully that no one got hurt from the earlier violence.

Honestly, it's hard to even remember or perhaps I am just trying to block those painful memories of how it used to be before TiVo. In the post-TiVo world, if I wanted to I could record any episode of Gilligan's Island and fast-forward to the end to see if, this time, they did get off the island. Almost as great is the ability to never miss a sporting event, while also having the time to be an involved parent and attentive husband. Yes, TiVo has allowed me to watch more sports and be a better dad and husband! Pinch me, my love affair with this special something, I like to call my "sweet little TiVo," seems too good to be true.

Chapter 11

Fanatic

A friend overheard me complaining to her husband that "I was so exhausted from the west coast trip." When she later asked me about "my trip," it took me a few seconds to understand why she thought I might have been traveling, but then explained that the Yankees had been playing on the west coast and the games don't start until 10:00 EST. Of course, with TiVo, I start the west coast games sometime between 11:00 P.M. and Midnight, skip commercials and any other breaks in the action, and catch up to "live" when the game ends at around 1:30 A.M.

TiVo has allowed me to catch about 152 of the 162 regular season Yankee games — the other ten and home playoff games I catch "live and in person" at Yankee Stadium — while not missing many family obligations nor shirking my parenting or husbandly responsibilities. One of the very few home playoff games that I missed, since I started sharing season tickets with friends in 1997, was "against my will and under protest." It was during the 1999 American League Championship Series against Boston. I had to attend a wedding for someone that my wife grew up with, but who has not lived in the United States for the past ten years or so and we have seen perhaps twice during such time.

Random Aside

What is more perfect than a summer wedding? When my wife suggested that we plan our wedding in August (of 1993), I thought and said "that would be perfect!" To be sure, I was thinking that in the summer the days are long and sunny and my wife would look so beautiful (as she did) in those outdoor wedding pictures and there would be no chance of snow related problems. Also, however, I believe that when planning a wedding (or any big event) one should consider potentially devastating sports scheduling conflicts. Major League Baseball's Playoffs make weddings in October and early November tricky; the NFL season and Playoffs make November, December, January and the first week of February problematic; and the NCAA's "March Madness" means that March and the first week of April could create a conflict. In other words, as I said, summer weddings are always wonderful! The weather is nice, the days are long and there are no major sports conflicts.

Look, even if you don't like sports, you have to understand that if you book your wedding on Superbowl Sunday or during the MLB Playoffs or Final Four, you will lose many of your guests. Some brave people will refuse to attend, causing some relationships to end.

> *Others, fearing a trip to the dog house with their significant other, may attend (albeit kicking and screaming even more than they would have if there was no sports conflict) and generally will not be happy to be there. Also, at these "sports conflicted events" many will migrate to a lounge, if there is one, to watch the game, instead of focusing on the "wonderful" event. It is something to think about when you are planning the big day.*

Well, I was, to be honest, not very happy to be at this wedding in 1999. It was nothing against the very nice couple. In fact, the husband is not even from the U.S., so I did not even blame him (very much) for not focusing on the sports programming conflict issue. But all of this is besides the point, the only television nearby was a small black and white one that the valet guys had in their booth and that I saw during only the handful of times that I went to check on my car. Otherwise, I was forced to surreptitiously listen in for scores with an earpiece connected to a walkman in my jacket pocket. I looked like a Secret Service guy with the disguised wire and earpiece — I would mockingly talk into my wrist and say things like; "tweed jacket, twelve o'clock, take him out!"

It is times like this — when you have to go with your wife to a wedding and have to give up your ticket to a Yankee/RedSox playoff game — that your single friends leave voicemails where they laugh and say things like "make sure you take note of every detail of the wedding because I am just dying to know ... Hah, Hah, Hah ... Sucker!" My wife never understands how men remember excruciating details about particular sporting events from years ago, but these events are like weddings for us and the statistics are like wedding details that my wife remembers — what they wore and what we ate and what song the couple danced to? I wish we could just understand each other better.

There are few places that I would rather be than at Yankee Stadium on game day (I even prefer it over attending weddings). And, perhaps since the Giuliani administration, Yankee Stadium has become the safest place in the city, perhaps in the nation, on game day. There seems to be one cop for every few fans and the area around the stadium is much less scary than it used to be. I recall in the late 1980s driving near the stadium and seeing a woman using a fire hydrant as a bidet — in broad day light. It was not a pretty scene, nor thankfully the type of detail usually provided by the commentators announcing the game. Truth be told, some sports commentators don't even provide much useful information about the actual sport they are covering.

Random Aside

Commentators that are former coaches are still referred to as "coach" by their colleagues in the broadcasting booth, much the way former Judges or Presidents are forever referred to with such titles. I'm not saying the former coaches have not earned the respect to be so referred ... I'm just saying.

Wouldn't it be nice if more commentators would try to teach some of the finer points of the game to casual viewers, rather than saying things like "if the Bruins don't make their shots, it will be tough for them to win this basketball game!" Really? You mean they keep score and if you don't get more points than your opponent, you lose?! What insight.

During the 2006 Final Four, much of America was introduced to a fun-loving guy named Glen Davis who played for LSU. The announcers explained that Davis, at 6'9" and over 300 pounds had the nickname (apparently since he was little) of "Big Baby." It sounded so strange to hear things like "they get the ball into 'Big Baby' and 'Big Baby' slams it home!" Referring to Davis by his nickname sounded much sillier somehow than say, calling Ervin Johnson "Magic," although perhaps this is because I had become accustomed to hearing about the exploits of one Magic Johnson. It made me wonder, though, if these announcers would call a player by any nickname that they may have been given in their life, no matter how silly? How about "Little Poopy" or "Stinky?"

I am sure you have heard some commentators report that an athlete is out of the lineup because he has "*a* knee" or "*a* hamstring." When I hear an injury report like this, two things always come to mind. First, when and why did they start reporting injuries this way. Second, he only has *one* knee or *one* hamstring! It must be tough to play with only one of those. Yet, even though there may be, for example, only one "Ben Roethlisberger" or "Eli Manning," commentators often say things like (in this example, when discussing young elite quarterbacks): "You've got your Ben Roethlisbergers and your Eli Mannings." If it wasn't so unintentionally amusing, it would be enraging.

I also really enjoy the way a great play or attribute of an athlete can be described with an otherwise negative word — this has been going on even before people starting saying "bad," but meaning "good." Like when commentators describe a pitcher's curveball as "just nasty" or "filthy" — and this was before pitcher Kenny Rogers was caught with a "filthy" hand that many believe was evidence that he was using a foreign substance to gain an unfair advantage. In football, players are positively referred to as "freaks" or "dogs," especially when they make a big tackle — i.e., deliver a "sick hit" or "big stick" or "jack someone up."

Random Aside

Now, as you can probably tell, I fully understand people that are big fans of their teams, but I do think that face painting by grown men is a bit much. If you and some buddies paint your face or chest as a goof during college or a college girl paints her school's logo on her cheek for a big game, that is one thing, but the father of three with his head and chest painted is over the top. The thing is that these "extreme" fans blend in with other crazy fans at the game (like freaks on Halloween), but on the way to or from the game (when mixed in with the general population) they look really scary.

A few years ago I took my wife to see an Aerosmith concert (she is a fan) when they were playing at Madison Square Garden. We had some time to kill before the show and my wife wanted a cup of coffee so we stopped into one of six Starbucks a few blocks away from the Garden. We were sitting in the back having coffee and I looked up to see a strange looking man in his forties walking past us to an empty table. The guy's face was painted white, he was wearing bright red lipstick and had a black star painted around one eye! As I am wondering what was wrong with this guy (it was not Halloween), I remembered that the band Kiss was the opening act for Aerosmith. This guy probably felt "normal" and like he "fit in" when he was at the concert with

> *other face-painted Kiss groupies. Yet, alone and out of context (much like the face-painted football fan at the gas station before the game) is really how the rest of us view these face painters whenever or wherever we see them.*

Before playoff games fans are treated to visuals and words that they don't often get to enjoy, such as the "unfurling" of a large American Flag. Does the word "unfurl" have any other uses besides the careful unfolding of a large flag? (At the risk of sounding unpatriotic, I could see an alternative use of the term in the adult film context). Also, nothing says playoff atmosphere, nor adds to the playoff "buzz" (besides the beer), then when the stadium is decorated with "bunting." When there is bunting and unfurling, athletes really must "step up" and "get in the zone," while making sure to still "take one game at a time," "take what the other team gives them," and "play within themselves," otherwise the game could "get away from them" and they could start to "press" and "overanalyze," rather than just "reading and reacting" and "being the ball." Because really the game plan is often rather simple: they just need to "put up some points" and play "solid defense."

Of course, for today's professional and big-time college athletes, "stepping up" or giving it his/her "all" or 100% is simply not enough — it's so 20th Century. Top athletes in the 21st Century routinely pledge to give their teams and fans at least the obligatory "110%." A promise of anything less would be downright insulting and akin to "loafing," particularly for fans willing to forgo sleep to follow their teams' away games in other time zones. Undoubtedly, this current level of commitment will soon seem insignificant in this arms race of unattainable goals — and the truly committed athlete will promise and expect 115% of themselves and teammates or maybe even 120%! Imagine how hard it will be for an athlete to give more than his all — particularly at the 115-120% level — when he has "a knee" or "a hamstring."

PART THREE

Love and Marriage (and Relationships): You Can Have One Without the Others

Chapter 12

It is a Small World After All!

It does seem like a small world sometimes, especially if you have grown up in the New York area as so many people's lives seem to crisscross through NYC — whether they are originally from the tri-state area and end up working or living in the City or whether they are transplants from other parts of the country, or the world, who spend some time living or working in the City. Running into someone who you knew back when or someone who was a college roommate of an old friend or who happens to know and hate a former back-stabbing girlfriend or whatever is always neat, although I contend that there is no one who enjoys the funny coincidence or "small world" story more than my mother.

My mom might as well have won the lottery when she recently ran into the mother of one of my wife's best friends growing up. Of course, Jewish grandmothers from the New York area who now live in Florida running into other Jewish grandmothers originally from the New York area who now live in Florida, should not be that much of a shocker. This is an especially unremarkable event when you consider that probably seventy-five percent of these people are confined to the Boca, Boynton Beach and West Palm Beach areas of Florida and all eat at the same three buffet restaurants during the hours of 3:00 P.M. and 5:00 P.M.

When it comes to "small world" stories, my mom loves them so much that she will connect seemingly unrelated events into yet another "just, wonderful" story. Like the time she was amazed when she met a woman that had a son named Jonathan and a daughter named Robin, which as she explained would have been my brother Robert's name had he been a girl! What a small world! She is particularly excited anytime she meets someone who shares a name (or whose family members or relatives no matter how distant share a name) with Robert or me or our wives or kids. Years ago I met a guy named Jason whose middle name was Scott. Why is this so remarkable? Well, though these are really common names, they also happen to be the middle names of my brother and I. I immediately called my mother to tell her this "amazing" story, but made sure she was sitting down before I broke the news. She found the tale so "unbelievable" that she thought I was just teasing her again about how small the world has become.

Random Aside

I have always tortured my mom — in a fun-loving sort of way — so that sometimes even when I am telling her a real amazing "small world" story, she is skeptical. One thing that I have done to her over the years concerns the fact that my brother and I sound nearly identical on the phone — it is really a small world because we come from the same mother and have the same phone voice. I have called my mom pretending to be my brother and sometimes he has called as me. On one occasion, he was over my apartment and I called my mom as him and then, in mid-sentence handed the

> *phone to my brother and then he handed it back to me in mid-sentence a few minutes later, all the while my mom thought that she was only talking to my brother. Then I (as my brother) told my mom that I (Jon) wanted to say hello. I paused and then said hello and then passed the phone back to Rob mid-sentence again. Now, I fully recognize that this type of torture will come back to me in spades from my kids years from now, but I just chalk this up to being part of the circle of life.*

Now, how could I make up something as crazy and improbable as a guy named Jason Scott? I think that years later, although skeptical, my mom has finally come around to believe this story — but I am not certain. My mom also really loves the true, yet amazing coincidence that my friend named "Scott" shares a birthday with her. And Scott's initials are SAM, like my daughters name! What are the chances?

My mom loves to tell me (at least annually) how my name was almost "Ass." Well, actually A.S.S. was almost my initials that would have been monogrammed on my shirts and briefcases for the rest of my life. It is not that I own many monogrammed items, but rather that I assume that friends and family would buy me monogrammed stuff for every occasion if my initials were A.S.S. — at least, that is what I would probably do if I knew an A.S.S. As my mom tells the story, she and my father had decided that my middle name would be Scott (perhaps the last thing they ever agreed upon) and had temporarily settled on Andrew for my first name. Then there was the epiphany when she realized that my initials would be ASS and they decided to name me ... Alex instead (okay, Jonathan). While it is certainly possible that it was my mom that recognized that my initials would be A.S.S. before it was too late, I suspect that it was in the context of a "small world" revelation. Perhaps she knew someone whose initials were shockingly close to what mine was going to be, like A.S. or A.S.T. or perhaps she thought it coincidental that I had an ass and now my initials would be A.S.S. too?

The other story that my mother loves to tell, not just to others, but to me repeatedly as if I just met her, is the "wonderful bicycle story." I was perhaps eight or nine-years-old and my mom had a garage sale (so she could get rid of junk she had accumulated to make room for the "new" junk she was always buying from other people's garage sales). Near the end of the sale, I decided that I would try to sell my bicycle — sure enough (in what my mom describes as a "miracle") ten minutes later someone pulled up with their grandkid and bought my bicycle for $36.00. That was sort of a coincidence to my mom — I guess much in the way that every sale involves someone who wants to buy an item and someone who wants to sell the item. Things got *really* crazy, however, when the very next week we were visiting some cousins and one of them, a teenage boy, indicated that he wanted to sell his ten speed bicycle. After a tough negotiation, he agreed to sell the bike for $25 dollars ($11 less than the bike I sold at the garage sale that had "no speeds," so I figured I did alright).

The best coincidence of them all, however, came almost a year later when I jumped off a curb on this bicycle and nearly killed myself when the frame actually came apart — the horizontal "ball-busting bar" came apart from the vertical section that holds the handlebars.

Random Aside

Given the male "equipment," why would they make men's bicycles with that bar and women's bike's without the bar? I know that we are now used to seeing it that way and it looks funny when a man is on a women's bicycle, but whose sick idea was it to place that horizontal bar in harm's way like that in the first place! I would like some answers and I would like them now.

I survived the crash, but the best part was that, as it turned out, (in some type of small world scenario) the bike was from Sears and they had a lifetime warranty on their bicycle frames. We brought it into Sears and I received a brand new bicycle, which at the time had a retail value of around $125.00. My mom just loves that story for all of the small world moments that she (and only she) recognizes and because I parlayed my crappy bicycle into a brand new bike with some cash left over and a few scrapes. There is another small world part to this story that *I* appreciate — the Sears bicycle brand was called "Free Spirit," which is one of the ways to describe my mom.

Chapter 13

"You Had to be There!?"

Why are some stories (be them small world stories or not) only funny if you were there? These are stories that, for some strange reason, simply don't "re-tell" well. Is this like whether a tree falling in a forest with no one around makes a sound? If you were not "there," does that mean the situation was not funny or does this have more to do with the way we experience humor? To be sure, the true test of whether something is really funny is if you laugh out loud when you are alone watching television or reading a book (hopefully this happens a few times when reading this book).

Laughter is "contagious," as they say and often amusing moments that we experience with friends are much funnier than they would be if we were alone. Also, these moments become fond memories that we look back on for years and years.

Random Aside

Sometimes when a good friend or family member starts laughing over nothing you start laughing too and, for the life of you, you cannot stop. These are not necessarily "had to be there" moments so much as they are random cases of the giggles.

A few years ago my brother and I were getting some "training" on a new phone system that was being installed in our law firm, and the technician was walking us through the process of recording new personal voice mail greetings. My brother got only a few words into his greeting, when I started belly laughing — for no apparent reason — and before long neither of us could control ourselves. (We might as well have been six and eight again and reacting to an older relative cutting one loose — or we might as well have been in our thirties when this happened, I suppose.) We had to leave the room to give the other even a remote chance of recording the greeting in one (more) try without laughing.

Unfortunately, I think as we get older and life gets complicated by adult responsibilities, we are unable or do not allow ourselves to let loose often enough that we routinely laugh over nothing.

Okay, I will now share a few "had to be there" stories — even though you were not there — that at the time had all people involved laughing hysterically. Many years later the people involved are still talking about these stories, although given that you were not there, perhaps you should just skip to the next chapter (I think it is a good one).

Here it goes. A few years ago I attended a friend's "wedding" in Tokyo with two single friends of mine. My two friends and I and the groom all at one point worked together and we are still close. By the way, I refer to the event as the "wedding," out of respect to one of my travel buddies who insists that the wedding was a sham because it was "officiated" by the bride's uncle who was not an "official" of any kind and because the couple did not get legally married until almost a year later in New York, but be that as it may.

One night my friends and I, along with a few of the groom's friends were bar hopping in an area called Roppongi, which if you are not familiar is a strange collection of good restaurants and bars/night clubs, some big business headquarters and some gentlemen's clubs.

As we were walking between bars, there were guys who would very aggressively try to encourage our group to come to the gentlemen's clubs they were hawking to see their beautiful dancers. Every guy sold his place as having the most beautiful, talented dancers in the world. Of course, we were very skeptical because usually any place be it restaurant, bar or club that is so great does not need some guy selling it so hard. After showing no interest, a few of these guys implored us to come and just take a peek without paying the cover charge — no obligation — and if we did not agree that they had the most beautiful and talented dancers in the world then we should simply leave. At my friends' insistence, of course, we went to a few places to check them out.

The routine went like this: We would walk in, do a lap around the place, as we looked in horror at just how untalented and frankly unattractive the dancers were and we would finish our lap by heading straight out the door we came in. Truth is that this became very amusing — comparing what was being advertised to the reality. Remember "The Gong Show" or the really bad auditions for "American Idol" — it is clearly more entertaining, from an unintentional comedy standpoint, when the "talent" has none at all. This scene was repeated multiple times between many bar stops during the course of a very late night out and seemed to get funnier each time — seven guys walking single file into these places and just as quickly exiting with facial expressions that looked as if we had just bit into a lemon or smelled a skunk. And just so you understand how bad things were, the alcohol did not even make the "talent" seem any more "talented."

Later that night, yet another guy approached our group on the street, trying to get us to take a free look at his establishment. Without thinking I said, "Sorry, we JUST can't take the chance." These seven words that just spilled out of my mouth without much thought, made all of us laugh so hard that we were crying — and we still laugh (although not as hard) when someone brings it up. What "chance?" We had nowhere to go or be at that late hour. The gentlemen was asking us to take two steps to our right and peek in a club to see if we agreed with him that it was a haven for talent. We were truly risking absolutely nothing, except being horrified once again by the lack of talent.

Now, if you enjoyed that story, then I am truly glad. If you did not, then perhaps it proves the "had to be there" point. (It really is a win/win for me either way). Or perhaps you thought the last story was as entertaining (or not) as the rest of this book, but this was the only time where I properly managed your expectations?

One more "had to be there" story. I was in law school and my wife (my fiancé at the time) and I were moving into a new apartment in New York City. My brother was helping us move and we had to pick up stuff from my in-laws house (some of which has, at this point, been moved four times and is sitting in my garage). My brother and I brought a moving truck to my in-laws house the night before the move so we could get an early start. Overnight there was some cold weather and some "black ice" had developed on my in-law's driveway, but who knew?

The next morning my mother-in-law stepped out of her front door and down the path to her driveway to move a car so that we could pull the truck up against the garage. She got a few steps down the driveway when her legs slipped out from under her on the black ice and she flopped down on the pavement. I was just exiting the house at this time and thinking she might be hurt I moved quickly towards her, knowing nothing of the black ice (a.k.a. secret coating of slippery stuff that makes you fall on your butt when you least expect it). I started to slip and slide and within moments, SPLAT! — I too hit the ground hard. I am now on my hands and knees crawling, like a puppy on ice, over to my mother-in-law who is on the ground near the driver's side door.

Thankfully, she seemed fine, but just then we hear the front door open and my brother — a very big guy — says, "Where are you guys?" as he steps out of the house. From our vantage point on the ground, with the car blocking much of our sight, all we can see of my brother is from his chest up and he apparently could not see us at all. Before we could warn him, we hear him yell "WHOA!" and we see his upper body disappear from our sight quickly as he slams the pavement. We then hear what sounds like a really large cat trying to gain a grip with his paws as he slips down an icy roof — "KUUUUURRRRR" — and see my brother sliding on his butt slowly down the driveway past us all the way to the street. Everyone was okay and scrambled back into the house, on our hands and knees, as we all started hysterically laughing. All this time my wife had been upstairs getting dressed and as she overhears us explaining what happened to my father-in-law, she starts laughing, which turns to wheezing and crying for the next twenty minutes. I suppose my wife was so close to the action that she did not "have to be there" to enjoy the story — she was "almost" there.

The people involved in these "had to be there" stories remember the details of the event years later and not just if they are starved for humor. The Japan trip was in 2004; the black ice incident was in 1992.

Okay, one more for those who (for some strange reason) have not skipped to the next chapter. This story goes back to around 1986, when I was a junior in high school and I can still remember all of the details. A fellow junior and I were at a party when a friend who I played football and lacrosse with — who was a senior with a car suggested that we leave the party and go with him and another guy to a comedy club in Manhattan. It sounded good to us.

While waiting in line a club employee suggested that we give the maitre de "a little something" and he would put us up front. As I was reaching to hand the maitre de a five dollar bill, he said sternly, "wrong denomination." My friends and I then pooled some money and I handed over twenty-five dollars, which got us a table that was not all the way in the back.

We were enjoying the show and the two drink minimum and these really small bowls of popcorn, which were very salty, but tasty. The staff seemed very attentive too, as they replaced our little popcorn bowls faster than we could finish them. The night seemed to be going very well, until we got the check. Apparently, there was a cover charge that was ten or fifteen dollars a person, plus the cost of the two drinks each and it turns out that those ten to twelve little bowls of popcorn, which we assumed were free, were seven dollars each! Our eyes widened as we passed around the bill and emptied all of our pockets trying to scrounge up enough cash. After we each cleaned out our wallets and pockets, we were still about forty or fifty dollars short. At this point, I noticed the waiter and manager — who had been watching us — talking and getting more and more agitated. The manager came over and started letting us have it and suggested that he was going to call the cops. Then, like cornered rats we (seventeen and eighteen year olds) struck back. I opened my mouth, and with considerable attitude, said to the manager: "I think you are running some kind of scam here! First, we have to pay twenty-five dollars just to get a decent seat in this place, then the cover charge, the drink minimums and BY THE WAY, where does it state that these tiny little bowls of popcorn are seven dollars each!"

The manager pretended to be surprised by our payoff of the maitre de (who I am sure regularly "kicks up" to the manager). He waved over the maitre de and asked him to give us back our twenty-five dollars. The money was returned to us, but I will never forget how red faced and mad the guy got — he was muttering to himself all manner of profanity, as he handed us the money and then said loudly that we should never, ever, come back to the place. I took the money and with a smartass smile said, "Thank you," as I handed the money to the manager.

Even after the maitre de "rebate," however, we were about twenty - thirty dollars short. Then my friend who drove us there, who had been calm and quiet the whole time, stepped in to the fray. In a very soft and slow manner, he said, "Sir, I come from a very influential family [his family owned many businesses in New York City] and this is a personal embarrassment to me and my family. I am going to give you my name, address and phone number and I will be back here tomorrow to repay what we owe." He gave the guy his real contact information, which blew us away, but I am not sure if he ever returned.

And with that we were released from the comedy place, without police intervention, and headed to my friend's car to drive back to Long Island.

Random Aside

Speaking of police intervention, I believe my first real interaction with law enforcement was when I was about nine while staying in Montauk, Long Island with the family of one of my oldest and closest friends Adam Perry Lang. Adam and I went to fish off a local dock one morning, perhaps a mile or two walk from where we were staying. Adam's mom had apparently thought we would be back for lunch (probably because we told her we would be back for lunch), but we were having fun and, I suppose, the time got away from us. At about 3:00 P.M., we left the dock and were heading home with our catch down a quiet road, when a police car slowly approached. A very serious looking and sounding officer said: "Are you Adam?"

With that I approached the car and noticed that the officer had a photo of the "perp" (apparently supplied by Adam's mom). Excitedly, I said, "Look Adam, he has your picture and everything!" The officer, who had gotten his men (or boys), didn't think this waste of time was very funny, but Adam and I still do.

We were all laughing really hard as we began the drive home, until we noticed the sign for the Midtown Tunnel toll. Uh oh! I think it was maybe two or three dollars, but there was no EZ-Pass back then and we did not have a dollar between us. My friend stopped the car in the middle of two lanes, about ten yards before the toll booths, and we searched in every crack between and under the seats of the car for loose change. We found a few coins, but still needed more than a dollar for the toll. There is really nothing like seeing four teenagers from Long Island panhandling out of their car in front of the toll booths for the Midtown Tunnel. A car full of teenage girls eventually gave us the money we needed, but no phone numbers.

My friend then threw the car into reverse to get back into a toll booth lane and almost ran over a short man who worked at the Midtown Tunnel and was trying to figure out what the heck we were doing. The man narrowly escaped serious injury and cursed us out pretty good. We paid the toll and all breathed a sigh of relief as we felt like we were now finally on our way home. We laughed some more as we sped down the highway, seemingly home free until a few minutes later when one of my friends yelled, "OH SHIT!" as he noticed that little red light on the dashboard below the "E"! With all the evening's distractions no one realized that we were so low on gas and the gas gauge showed that we were running on fumes. My friend began shifting the car between park and neutral to conserve gas and we literally coasted back to Long Island. What a memorable night, but then again perhaps you just had to be there.

Chapter 14

Fishing for the Invite and Other Wedding Fun

Like many men I struggle to understand women, including just how much some of them seem to love everything associated with weddings. In the months leading up to their wedding, women will receive strange calls from friends that they have not been in touch with for years. These old friends are often fishing for an invitation to the wedding, trying to re-inject themselves into an engaged couple's life in the hopes of making the wedding list cut. Men never do this. In fact, men may actually avoid calling engaged people with whom they are not very close — fearing that they might then make "The List." Don't get me wrong, a wedding is a wonderful event to be a part of, assuming it involves someone with whom you are close.

Creating the wedding list is one of the most stressful parts (of the many stressful parts) of the lead up to the wedding for an engaged couple. My suggested approach, which I do not think is followed by many women and certainly was not followed by my wife, is to invite only the people with whom you really want to share the day and who you are sure really want to attend. I did not want anyone to attend my wedding out of some sense of obligation. This is also my approach (or attempted approach) when responding to a wedding invitation. My argument to my wife (almost always a loser) is that we should not have to go to a wedding for a couple that we barely know just because we are invited. I figure the couple would be much happier if they did not have to pay for our dinner, but we still sent them a nice gift.

In compiling our list, my wife (and I assume she is not alone) felt we had to invite anyone who invited us to their wedding. I was concerned that inviting a real fringe friend or family member who was not yet married might cause them to invite us to their wedding someday and, of course, my wife would then insist that we attend that wedding too. It is a vicious cycle, this wedding thing.

Once you are done with the wedding list stress, it is time to start fighting over the seating chart. Can you seat certain people together or are they not talking again? Where do we put the group of elderly relatives who will complain that it is too loud if they are placed anywhere near the band? Of course, when we anticipate the elderly relative seating concern and seat them at the other end of the room, they then complain that they are too far away from the action. "It's like they left us to die in Siberia!"

Random Aside

Probably a good rule of thumb for wedding planning, and relationships in general, is to choose your battles. I really didn't care too much about many choices, like flowers, invitations, linens, the cake, favors for bridal party, etc. and would help my wife choose, when asked, between the two or three alternatives that she was considering. The wedding band and the music played was another story. My wife and I met

> *with the band and went over the music they would play and made it very clear to them not to take requests from older relatives, who were liable to request that the band play some truly awful songs (like bad pop music from ten years earlier that they think is the "hot" "new" music that the "kids are listening to today"). To insure clarity on this issue, I went so far as to create a "Hit List" for the band, explaining that if they played any songs on that list, I might hit them. It included every painful song that I had been tortured with on the Bar Mitzvah circuit in the 1980's, such as "We are Family," "Celebration," " Hot, Hot, Hot," and anything involving synchronized dancing or clucking like a chicken. With clear rules in place, I think everyone was happy and things didn't get ugly.*

Some couples fight over whether there will be a bachelor party (of course there will be) or the parameters for it. Some guys claim not to want a bachelor party, although some of these guys just fear their soon-to-be-wife's wrath. If there isn't a bachelor party, however, the wrath of the bachelor's friends can be as bad or worse, and can be summed up like this: "What do you mean you don't think you want a bachelor party!? You selfish prick, don't you understand that the bachelor party is not for you? It's for us, your married friends who need an excuse to get away for a weekend in Vegas!"

After all the pre-wedding fun, the big day provides no shortage of special "moments." Wedding speeches and other special wedding surprises can provide a great deal of comedy, intentional or otherwise. One of my all-time favorite wedding speeches was given by a relative of the groom who managed to say absolutely nothing at all while speaking for a full twenty minutes. He started by explaining that, when he was struggling to decide what to say in his speech, he wondered what one particular dead relative might have suggested that he say. Then he wondered what a different dead relative would have suggested that he say. Then he thought maybe he would talk about this. Then he thought maybe he should talk about that. Then he considered talking about an entirely different topic, but thought better of it. He concluded his non-speech by making a toast that went something like, "Please raise your glasses and toast the bride and groom. Marriage is not easy, so good luck." So the guy discussed all the various speech topics that he considered, while never actually saying anything about any of the rejected topics and failing to mention the actual topic of his speech — not having a clue what he should say. What a memorable moment, for me anyway.

Other truly memorable wedding moments involve musical and/or dance numbers performed by guests, rather than paid entertainers. On one such occasion, the mother of the bride came out during the reception in a light blue sequined dress that she had changed into specifically for the performance. She sang a Broadway show tune and even used props (including a hand-held mirror that she sang into at times for dramatic effect) as she belted out the song while prancing around the dance floor. The performance was extremely painful, not because the woman couldn't sing (she actually had a decent voice), but rather because she took herself so seriously and because of her theatrics. To make matters worse, the bride, who appeared to be tone deaf, followed her mother with a song of her own. These wonderful unintentional comedic moments are thankfully preserved on video for years and years of future enjoyment.

My favorite scene in our wedding video involves our videographer's apparent "interest" in a young attractive female guest, who is a friend of mine that I grew up with on Long Island. On a few occasions, the video slowly panned up and down on this woman and then got a good close-up shot of her from behind as she walked past the camera. It was like the videographer (who, by the way, had his wife there as an assistant) forgot that he was looking through a camera, enabling the viewer to watch, through the videographer's eyes, the "undressing" of our guest. I suppose one of the risks for women interested in attending (yet another) wedding, is the possibility that they may be "featured" in the video.

Every wedding attended by at least one elderly Jewish couple has a scene in the wedding video that goes something like this (just change the names of the parties): The videographer passes the microphone to an eighty year-old named Murray Rabinowitz to see if he wants to record a message for the bride and groom. Murray, looking a little dazed, quickly passes the microphone to his wife, Gertie, who cannot grab it fast enough. She clutches the microphone tightly with both hands, presses it up against her mouth and shouts, with a deep raspy voice that sounds like she has smoked for fifty years of her life:

> *Is it on?! Is it on?! Oh, the red light means it's on! Murray and I want to wish you all the best of everything! You two look BEAUTIFUL! What a BEAUTIFUL affair! The food is great ... what a smorgasbord! Stevie, I remember your Bar Mitzvah like it was just yesterday. You are still that sweet little boy, only a little heavier and with not as much hair. And Jennifer, you look gorgeous! And so thin — I hear you lost more than 30 pounds! Well, I think that's wonderful. Keep it up. Best of luck and all the happiness in the world to both of you. I cannot wait for you to have kids. You guys are DELICIOUS! Mazel Tov!*

After their video performances, many old relatives at wedding receptions seek out the bride and groom and say, usually very loudly and in their face, something like: "Do YOU know who I am!?" or "Do YOU know how we are related!?" I am often left wondering if they know the answers to these questions themselves. In any case, it appears that as people get older, being recognized and, perhaps, their legacy (such as it is) becomes more and more important.

Strange introductions at weddings are certainly not limited to senior citizens. At my wedding reception in 1993, I turned and started to walk to my right when I was startled by a short man, perhaps in his mid to late twenties, who had a huge ear to ear grin and was no more than a quarter of an inch from me as he almost screamed: "Hi, I'm your cousin, MELVIN!" Apparently, he was one of my wife's cousins who I had never heard about or seen before then and have not heard about or seen since. I was a bit flustered because he frankly scared the crap out of me and was really in my personal space. I believe I asked him (because of his close proximity) if he intended on kissing me, which confused him, and then I said, "Well, nice to meet you Melvin!," and moved on to greet another one of the guests that I would never see again.

I addressed this long-lost relative phenomenon during my "best man" speech at my brother's wedding by saying: "For those of you who have not seen me since my Bar Mitzvah (more than ten years earlier), I am Robert's younger brother, Jonathan." This was an ice-breaker, designed to make people laugh, as well as to seriously let many people know who was speaking. This remark also exposed a truth about weddings: Many extended family members and marginal friends who attend weddings — and simply could not be trimmed during one of the fights over "The List" — are, like Melvin, seen (perhaps with good reason) only once ... every decade or two.

Chapter 15

Kids in the ... House!

Although getting married is certainly a major milestone and life-changing event — with or without an entertaining video — it pales in comparison to having children. Everyone says that your life will never be the same after you have children and I found this to be true (in a good way). Apart from the new responsibilities, challenges, and wonderfully gratifying and proud moments, parenthood prompted me to look at the world differently, including trying to understand it from my children's perspective. What causes them, without prompting, to say and do some of the things they say and do — some of which are quite entertaining and some, well ... not so much. It is also fascinating to witness children experiencing for the first time things that have become routine to adults, and to hear their unbiased perceptions about the subject matter — before being socialized to understand or perceive something in a particular way.

Random Aside

Top Eleven Ways Becoming a Parent Will Change Your Life ("Eleven" because, if possible, it is always good to "crank it up to Eleven!"):

No. 11: This is the start of the daily battle not to become your parents.

No. 10: Once the apple of your eye, Fido finally gets demoted to "dog."

No. 9: Your in-laws now have many new things to be mad at you about — not because certain issues are really important to them, but because they "just want what's best" for you and your child.

No. 8: You start using words like "poopie" and saying "I wuv you" ... at work.

No. 7: People who never had kids, including the recently paroled guy who works at the video store, start giving you parenting advice.

No. 6: Bowel movements are timed, inspected and judged like an Olympic event.

No. 5: Five hours of sleep and only puked on once, is considered a "good night."

No. 4: You will become such an expert in the fine art of diaper changing that you may even consider entering a competitive diaper changing contest on ESPN6.

> *No. 3: You realize that all of your friends that you once thought were terrible parents, are, in fact,...* really *terrible parents.*
>
> *No. 2: You begin debating the merits of diaper rash ointments, stroller technology and which children's shows are more enjoyable for* you *to watch....*
>
> *No. 1: "Frequent" sex takes on a whole new, "less frequent" meaning.*

Our first child, Samantha, was born in 1998 (she requires that we call her Sami and just scolded me as she noticed her birth name being typed on my laptop). I remember her first pair of jeans — they were tiny versions of adult jeans with little back and front pockets, which I always thought was very convenient when my daughter was ten months old because if she didn't want to bring a handbag to her playdate, she could just carry her license, keys and lipstick in the pockets.

Although she and her tiny jeans were cute to me and most we came across, I learned quickly to recognize the people that simply do not like kids. There are some whose kids are grown and are disgusted when a two-year-old behaves as a curious two-year-old is supposed to behave. If you ask these child-haters they will swear that their child was always perfect, never had a tantrum — perhaps never took a crap in his or her diaper when it was not a convenient time. Some get huffy (which, as you should know is different than getting "salty") when, for example, a child is a little loud at 2:00 P.M. at a loud diner — not exactly 10:00 P.M. on a Saturday night at a place suitable for a romantic date.

Our son Matthew was born in early March of 2000. I was really rooting for a Leap Year birthday. Always thinking ahead, I thought it would give him a great rap with women in college. Think about it, he could saddle up to someone at a bar in 2020 and say, "Hi, I'm Matt, my friends and I are here celebrating my fifth birthday!"

Random Aside

When I told a woman I know that Matt just missed being a Leap Year baby by a few days, she said her kid had as well because he was born in late February — two years earlier! Of course, unable to "let it go" I felt obligated to explain that, actually, her kid had missed being a Leap Year baby by just four days ... and two years, given that it is a once every four year event. Boy, do I know how to burst someone's bubble!

Plus, as a Leap Year kid I thought I could explain to Matt, say in 2005 as we are heading to yet another of his classmate's birthday parties, that he would not be having another birthday party, nor would he be getting any birthday presents, until 2008, but "just think about how great it will be then, after waiting so long!" Okay, I was not really going to do that, although I truly did think the Leap Year rap would be great for him down the road.

As it turns out, however, Matt doesn't need any help with his rap, he has always had many "girlfriends" — such as they are — starting as early as his preschool and kindergarten classes. I remember the first time he told me, with a sheepish grin, that he had a "girlfriend" in his nursery school class. (We will refer to her here as Susan, the name of the cutest girl in my nursery school class who I was "caught" kissing under the table and who put green paint on my nose when I was flirting with another girl in the class and who is today a mother of four children and still a close friend). Matt mentioned his "Susan" a few times, but I had forgotten about the whole thing until I was in his classroom for a going away party that his class was making for him when we were leaving the City in the middle of the school year — he was about four and a half.

Random Aside

The cupcakes at this event did not disappoint, but made me wonder why it is that cupcakes are rarely served at adult functions? They are so tasty and such nice little handheld treats. Please if there is someone out there who has control over this kind of stuff, please encourage others to serve adults cupcakes too — is that so much to ask?

The class had made Matt a book with each kid coloring a page that also contained something that he or she had said about why they liked Matt or why he was their friend, which was transcribed by the teachers. I am doing a "reading" of the book to the class with Matt sitting next to me, and most of the kid's pages say things like, "I like Matt because he plays blocks with me, he's funny, etc." Then, halfway through the book, one of the pages says, "I like Matt because he is handsome," and was signed by Susan! I immediately look up (recalling that this was his little lady) and asked which one was Susan, but unfortunately she was out sick that day. Oh well, I thought.

As I was leaving and saying goodbye to the teachers, I noticed that the kids had attendance charts with their pictures on them and I look for Susan — this is the first girl that Matt had expressed any interest in and I wanted to see what kind of taste my little man had. I saw a picture of a little girl who was sort of cute, but not exactly what I expected. Hmm, I thought to myself and said to one of his teachers that he has been talking about this girl as I motioned to the picture. The teacher said, "Oh Susan is gorgeous," but she pointed out that the picture I was looking at was of a different girl in his class "who is cute too." Susan is the picture below — I was confused, as the names were above not below the pictures! Wow! This little girl had flowing long brown hair and big blue eyes and looked like she should be in a Gap commercial — she was stunning! Sorry, but I was very proud of Matt at that moment — any dad who is being honest would have been too. I was thinking "that's my boy!"

This was not my first "that's my boy!" moment with Matt. The first came when my wife was getting a sonogram and we were going to find out the gender of Matt the fetus. Usually, the fetus is curled up and the technician has to show you what is what and sometimes you just have to take their word for it — at least with the technology prevalent in 2000. As it happens, though, for just an instant during the sonogram, Matt the fetus had his legs spread eagle as if being frisked and "hello" he's "hanging like an 'adult' film star." I immediately screamed out, "That's my boy!" My wife who for some reason thought she was having another girl asked the technician if she was sure that it was a boy? "They don't have kickstands" is what I think I said and the technician gave my wife a look like "you're kidding right?"

We quickly learned just how different boys and girls are (beside the obvious anatomical differences). Matt from birth loved trucks and cars way more than Sami ever did. While this sounds unremarkable, it was not as if we pushed these items on him, nor did we keep them away from Sami. Sami has never been what one would describe as a Tom Boy, but she also has never loved dolls or dresses either. She would think it was cool when the local fire trucks would pass us on the street in New York City, but would never get nearly as excited as Matt who would insist that I take him to the nearby fire house on East 85th Street almost every weekend — they would often put him on the truck in the driver's seat and Matt would be all smiles.

Matt and his pre-school and elementary school buddies are obsessed with how fast and strong they are. Speed and strength are of critical importance to young boys. I remember this from the playground at my own elementary school. It is like men come out of the womb with some innate Darwinian survival of the fittest gene. When they are young they are ready to hunt and gather, although often not for food or anything else of any redeeming value.

For Matt, his first five years of life seemed to be a hunt for the attention of cute girls. (Of course, this too can be seen as innate Darwinian behavior). Whenever we would be in a public place he would find the cutest girl — usually between eight and sixteen-years old or even older and manage to get her attention and sometimes even hugs! When we were living in the City, one of my single friends would often ask whether Matt and I were available to get a bite to eat for lunch or early dinner at a local burger or Mexican place — Matt being the "chick magnet." Without fail, the waitresses would all come over to talk to Matt and women at neighboring tables would start talking to him, and I would often overhear them asking him things like, "Which one is not your dad?"

My friend has repeatedly asked me if he could "borrow" Matt for the day, as if he were an accessory, so he could take him to the park or wherever to assist in meeting women. I have to explain, again and again, that we do not "rent out" Matt like a party pony. Of course, I am happy to go somewhere with Matt and my friend, assuming it is appropriate for Matt and I (not this single friend) is responsible for Matt's care.

My daughter who has always been extremely precocious has played "wingman" of sorts on a few occasions, even though she might not have realized it. When she was about three, I was in Central Park on my bicycle with her on a kiddie seat on the back and we drove over to a grassy area to meet up with another single friend of mine. This friend, who I will refer to as Michael (because that is his name), is not that forward with women (he likes to sit back and wait and wait, and wait some more for them to come to him). We found Michael who had been lying out in the sun and after a few minutes of small talk with Sami, she noticed four young bikini-clad girls, just to the right of where Michael was sitting. Without any prompting, Sami, with her long curly blond hair and huge blue eyes, marched right over to the girls and said loudly and forcefully, to each in succession — with one hand on her hip and the other pointing at them: "What is your name? What is your name? What is your name? ...." They each sat up laughing and gave their names to this powerful little lady and then Sami said, motioning to us, "That is my dad and this is his friend Michael," and then in almost a scolding tone said, "Michael take your sunglasses off so they can see your face!" Of course, instead of thinking wow what an amazing ice breaker, let me run with it, Michael sheepishly said hello and stared down at his feet.

Like mother like daughter, I suppose because my wife has always been looking to set up my single friends. When we are out to dinner, Jill can always spot the people who are on a first date — maybe this is a woman thing. She is always so excited to observe the mating ritual of the human single person — it is like a Discovery Channel show — observing some rare breed of animal to see if they will mate.

About six months later, Sami and my wife and I were eating in a diner on the Upper East Side and in comes Derek Jeter with his sister and another friend. (Jeter, Jorge Posada and some other Yankees at one time had apartments near where we lived). From birth my kids have been watching Yankee games with me live or on television and they could recognize Jeter and many other players from very early on. As Jeter walked past our table, we all noticed him and my wife remarked how he was even better looking in person. Jeter and his party sat at the other end of the diner in the corner, with Jeter's back to most of the customers. There was definitely a buzz in the place, as many people noticed, but did not want to bother him.

My wife started asking Sami, every ten minutes or so, whether she needed to use the bathroom (so my wife could walk with Sami past Jeter's table). Eventually, to my wife's delight, Sami said she needed the bathroom and, surprise, surprise, my wife said she would take her. As they walked towards Jeter, I noticed many people stretching their necks and enviously watching the cute little girl approaching the sports icon. Sami stopped right in front of Jeter and said, "Aren't you Derek Jeter?" He smiled and said, "Yes I am" — Sami and my wife were beaming as Jeter (who was so nice to Sami and seemed like such a great guy) gave Sami a high five. Then, Sami (at three and a half) who seemed to recognize that many people in the diner were watching and envious, stretched her neck toward the onlookers, smirked and gave everyone a sarcastic one finger wave!

Traveling with kids (any further than the local diner) is hard enough without being singled out by airport security for the random search. This happened to us, when our kids were under four-years-old; we were called aside for the extensive search to determine, I suppose, if we were terrorists. After rifling through all of our carry-on bags, our diaper bag and all the compartments of our double stroller, the security forces that are making our country safe came across the most nefarious of objects — the bottle of formula. At this point, I was instructed to "drink the formula," I guess to make sure that it was not liquid explosives or poison. I should point out that they were nice enough to permit me to remove the rubber nipple bottle top before I took my taste. It would also have been nice if they would have burped me, but perhaps that is asking too much.

It would seem to make sense to use the limited resources mostly to search men, say between the ages of eighteen and forty, who do not have a kid in diapers with them. Families traveling with young children have enough trouble completing even the simplest of tasks; having toddlers in tow is hardly the recipe for smoothly executing a terrorist operation. But, what do I know.

While the bottle of formula was hardly a security concern, it reminds me of the time Sami tried to outsmart a child-proof bottle of children's vitamins. She was almost five-years-old and she wanted to open the bottle of vitamins that I had taken down from the cabinet but was struggling. "How come I can't open this thing," Sami said.

I explained that the bottle was made so that adults and not children would open it.

She then asked, "How does it [the bottle] know if you are a child?"

Doing my best to keep a straight face, I informed her that "you have to tell it your age." Sami turned her head slightly and shot me a questioning glance, as I picked up the bottle, looked into it and said "thirty-three" and opened the bottle with ease. "See!"

She seemed very, very skeptical, but just in case there was something to my tale — Sami took the bottle, looked around and spoke softly into the bottle "sixteen!" She was, however, still unable to open the bottle and looked a bit frustrated.

I explained that "you can't lie to the bottle" about your age. She just shook her head, with a sheepish grin. A few months later she happily pointed out to me that she could now read the directions on these bottles — where it says "push and turn." They are crafty, these little ones.

Young children, as everyone knows, can also be brutally honest. Everyone has their stories of a small child's inappropriate, yet honest assessments, such as "mommy that man is really fat," etc. A related issue is the way kids approach, for the first time, an objectively bizarre phenomenon that the rest of us have come to ignore.

When Matt was eight, we were watching a college lacrosse game on television when on the screen appeared a large graphic announcing "The Dick's Sporting Goods Player of the Game." Matt, seeing this, quickly spun his head toward me with a puzzled look, asking "Isn't that a *curse* word?!"

Trying to be delicate, I explained that "well, it is ... but it is also someone's name."

"HUH?!" Matt barked back with an even more confused look.

"I know Matt," I said, "There are some things in this world that really don't make much sense."

This experience left me thinking once again about how my kids perceive the world around them. It also got me thinking: Why would someone given the name Richard, decide..., "You know what, don't call me Richard or Rich or Richie or Joe, call me Dick!" Is this any more ridiculous than a man named Charles deciding he wants to be referred to as "Cock" or a Virginia, "Vagina?" Not really. Matt's instincts were dead on. Young children approach these absurdities much in the way a space alien might — objectively noting that which the rest of us have become numb to by years and years of exposure.

Chapter 16

Migrating to Boca

Many nearing retirement age, particularly Jewish people from the Northeast, feel obligated to, at least, consider relocating to Florida or at least buy a burial plot there. These are among the many things that change when you get old. A few years back my wife's Uncle (let's call him Jim) turned 70 years-old and at a surprise party for him I thought it would be nice to say a few words in his honor and about the new challenges that he was now facing. I began scribbling a roast on a piece of paper, when my wife noticed what I was up to and felt strongly that her family would find it more offensive than humorous. I still disagree, but you can be the judge. It went like this:

> *People always say "age is only a number," but when the number is 70 ... well, you're pretty damn old. Of course, Jim you don't look a day over 68 ..., and your dentures have never looked better. Jim you're at the age where your comb over or "swoop" is getting so thin that you need to start combing the hair from your ears and*

soon from your arm pits to cover your bald head. You all probably know that men stop growing, often by age 18, but their ears continue to grow a tiny amount throughout their lifetime. I think this is nature's way to ensure that there is enough surface area for the ever increasing ear hair.

I didn't realize that there would be quite so many old people here (and some even older than Jim) — everyone please turn to your right and if you think the person is being offended by these old age jokes, please lower the volume on their hearing aid.

Jim is at the age, and let's face it so are most of you, where bran replaces milk as one of the major food groups. I know I am not getting any younger either, but at this point Jim you have chunks of stuff in your colon older than me. Also you know you're old when lying about your age only makes you a younger senior citizen. Now when Jim arrives at an event people are careful not to say, "Glad you made it," but instead say, "Good to see you."

Each decade men tend to wear their pants an inch higher, until their nipples get chaffed by their belt. Ah the circle of life — both ends involving the use of diapers. Of course, one of the big differences between being a baby and an old man is that when you were little your family praised you when you were potty trained — Jim soon your family will actually be proud of you when you are trained to poop in your diaper.

Seriously though, Jim ... you are really old. And many of the people here today, who actually know where the hell they are, really love you.

Everyone, please raise your glass and toast to Jim a wonderful and distinguished older gentlemen.

Happy Birthday, old buddy!

As relatives like Jim get older and older, so do words in the English language — and some actually seem to pass away after a few generations stop using them. Examples of some "endangered" words are dungarees, valise, satchel, bathing trunks and chaise lounge (which seems to be making a comeback). Similarly, some names seem to pass away with your elder relatives. How many kids born recently are named Murray, Morris, Melvin, Gertrude, Sonia or Blanche? In contrast, some words are relatively new to the English language or vernacular, but have not yet caught on with older generations.

Years ago, my brother and I were visiting my late grandmother Dorothy in Florida (yes, in Boca) and my brother formed the word "sorbet" in the Scrabble game he was playing with my grandma. Grandma Dorothy then said loudly her trademark "OH, NO! That's not a word!" And then she barked: "GO get my dictionary in the front hall closet!" Of course, her Webster's Dictionary, was circa 1950, and sure enough it did not include "sorbet." With a satisfied grin Grandma played on. (My brother could not let it go and mailed my Grandma a sorbet advertisement the following week.)

My Grandmother Dorothy was not always the easiest to deal with and that is being charitable. Until she moved to the Century Village retirement community in Boca Raton in the early 1980s when I was twelve, she lived on the second floor of a three family house in Queens. My Great Aunt Ceil (the sister of Dorothy's husband Al) and her husband Great Uncle Eli, lived on the third floor and Great Grandma Sadie lived on the first floor. My great aunt and uncle (great in every sense of the word) moved first to Century Village in the early 1980s and then Dorothy followed shortly thereafter. Grandma Dorothy had been widowed approximately five years earlier and the conventional wisdom in my family was that Eli moved South to distance himself from Dorothy who got under his skin, like no one else — over the course of sixty years or so. "Century Village" was one of the earlier generations of Boca retirement communities — Boca Version 1.0 — or for "Seinfeld" fans the community could be referred to as "Boca Del Vista *Phase I*," rather than the "Phase II" where Jerry's parents lived.

During the 1970s, I recall my grandmother cooking massive quantities of tasty and very heavy food — like brisket and veal or chicken parmesan. She would always give everyone so much grief if they did not eat enough for four people. When I was perhaps six or eight years-old, Grandma Dorothy was after me to try her chopped liver (I feel like gagging just writing those words). I explained that I did not like chopped liver, but she was not satisfied with this response because "I had never tried it!" I explained to her that I had the unique ability to determine whether I will like something or not by simply smelling it and the smell of chopped liver clearly indicated that I would not like it. She did not accept this response. Rather than have her try to force feed it to me, I told her that if it would really make her happy I would try it, but warned that I would not like it. She then shoved a big heaping tablespoon of the stuff in my face. I took a small taste and immediately grabbed some napkins and all but puked it up and continued gagging and spitting, as if I had unwittingly tasted poop. Of course, she was now angry and got even more so after I said, "I told you I wouldn't like it."

Random Aside

This reminds me of when people ask you a question, but really only want to hear one answer. Do I look like I lost weight? Do I look fat in these jeans? Don't you just love this new outfit? My problem is that I have never been good at telling people what they want to hear. I implore people not to ask me any questions, unless they want my true feelings and then only if there will be no repercussions for giving my honest response. Of course, people continue to ask these kinds of questions and even if they swear they want my honest opinion I manage to piss them off when I say, "Well, actually …."

When providing brutally honest assessments, people often temper their harsh words by prefacing their remarks — while unconsciously making a face that looks like a cross between showing concern and expecting to get hit — with phrases like, "Well, … actually;" "Honestly …;" or "To tell you the truth …." Sometimes in a similar attempt to "lessen the blow," unsolicited brutal honesty is tempered by prefatory phrases like: "Not for nothing, but …;" "I don't mean to be nosey, but …;" or "I know you didn't ask, but…."

Of course, "not for nothing" is hardly English (and is often followed by "six of one and half-a-dozen of the other;" "I'm on the job 24[hours] 7[days a week]," and other brilliant bits of wisdom), but is the perfect example of words whose

> *sole purpose is to introduce, yet temper a harsh remark. "Not for nothing, but you smell like you have not showered in days." See, when you say it that way doesn't it almost sound like a compliment? The email equivalent of this phenomenon is the use of ☺ to dull otherwise harsh words, such as, you are such a jerk, I hate you ☺!*

Most of my recollections of the difficult Dotty, surrounded food (perhaps this is just because as Jews most events in life just fill time gaps between the next meal). There was the last time she was ever in New York, when she stayed with us for a week on Long Island in June of 1982. We were having dinner and my father said to her, innocently I thought, "Can you please pass the carrots." This managed to set her off: "OH, Now I'm *'YOU,'* that's who I am!" I remember my brother, dad and I looking at each other with confused expressions and thinking, "What the heck just happened!

About eight years later, I was in college and during Spring Break instead of doing something fun, I agreed to go with my mother and brother down to Boca to visit Grandma. One night we attended a community Passover Seder at a local restaurant. We were seated at a large table with about twelve or fifteen complete strangers that also lived in her development. My brother, mother and I were three of the five people out of over a hundred in attendance that were under sixty-years-old. At the end of the meal there was a large tray of cookies that was passed around the table. As luck (in terms of unintentional comedy) would have it, the cookie tray was passed around the opposite end of the table first and when it made its way to us, I held it and asked, "Grandma, would you like a cookie?" This too set her off. She said (like everything else she ever said) loudly, "OH, NO" (pointing an accusatory finger across the table) "THEY, took all of the good ones!"

Random Aside

Lacking any public filter seems to be another aspect of the human condition that comes full circle, as one's "filter" seems to lose its effectiveness during the "golden years." Grandma Dorothy's inner monologue (no matter how insensitive or embarrassing) was offered regularly. She was also once on the receiving end of a truly memorable "unfiltered" comment. She was in the hospital and not doing that well and was visited by a relative (in his mid-seventies at the time and the poster-child of an unfiltered senior), who upon entering the hospital room said to Grandma: "After seeing you yesterday I thought we would be going to a funeral today." Grandma, in her own "I'm not dead yet moment" exploded with a loud: "WHAAATTT!!!"

The other memorable moment from this dinner involved the "parting gifts." Just before clearing everyone's main course, the entire wait staff was dispatched throughout the restaurant and began handing out sheets of aluminum foil and sandwich bags to everyone. They just assumed (correctly) that nearly every person would want to bring home their leftovers.

Grandma Dorothy often made me want to crawl in a hole. In hindsight, these are fond memories, but at the time, especially when I was a teenager or in my early twenties, these experiences were brutal. On that same trip, Aunt Ceil and Uncle Eli took all of us out for dinner to celebrate Grandma's birthday, which had been earlier in the week. She insisted we go to some place that was a cross between Friday's and Beefsteak Charlie's. In the lobby of the restaurant there was a big sign that said "Come in on Your Birthday and Your Dinner is on Us!" When the check arrived, Grandma told the waitress that it was her birthday and, thus, her meal should be free. The waitress asked if Dorothy's birthday was actually that day (and may have even "proofed" her). My grandma conceded that it was a few days ago, but explained that a friend took her to the place a year or two ago during the week of her birthday and her meal was free. The waitress apologized and explained that she couldn't give the free meal, unless it was actually grandma's birthday. "WELL, I NEVER! Send over the Manager," Grandma Dorothy barked, as my brother and I looked for yet another hole to crawl into. Eli's blood was boiling at this point, as he had seen this routine one too many times and he reminded Dorothy, loudly, that he was paying for dinner, so "WHAT'S THE DIFFERENCE!"

Even buying Grandma Dorothy a gift could prove challenging. During one of our visits to Boca, my wife presented Grandma with a pair of earrings. Upon opening the box, she made it clear that she did not like the gift — she began shaking her head and let out a softer spoken version of her famous "oh, no!" (She never seemed to subscribe to the "it's the thought that counts" adage.) My wife quickly pointed out that she would be happy to exchange the earrings for Grandma and asked her to describe the style she would prefer. To this Grandma "explained" that she wanted "IMPORTANT" earrings. Perhaps this meant that she wanted earrings that "important" people might wear or ones that would make her look "important?" Although this description was not exactly helpful for the return trip to the store, it was consistent with other inexact descriptions she used to describe her grandchildren: "delicious!"

Grandma Dorothy passed away in 2002 and she did not go down without a fight.

Random Aside

Some say that you should never discuss anything negative about those who have passed away, especially family members. While, I don't think it is necessary to stress negative things in a eulogy or to gratuitously pile on with criticism about the dead, at any time, I also don't think one should rewrite history. To be sure, Grandma Dorothy was a loving and loyal friend and family member. She certainly did, however, have a "prickly" side, which years later I believe those who knew her can, and should, recall and enjoy (perhaps even "celebrate"). Also, perhaps being featured in my book would have made her feel "important!"

In the last few years of her life, unfortunately she had many health problems, many involving circulation and her legs, and it was very difficult for her to get around. Various health professionals from a local state run agency were regularly visiting her to provide assistance, but apparently no one wanted to go back to help her after a few visits because they claimed she was too difficult to deal with. The agency was running out of new people to send to her and at one point started a proceeding to have her deemed incapacitated and placed against her will into a home, claiming that she was not allowing the agency to provide her the services she needed. My brother and I attended her commitment hearing where the lawyer who specializes in these matters that handled her case fought off the commitment by explaining the sad truth that she was not crazy, she knew exactly what she was doing, but was just very difficult. Essentially the winning argument was that (in America) you don't involuntarily commit someone and take away their liberty, just because they are a serious pain in the butt.

In 2005, my family went down to Florida to see my mom and Aunt Ceil and Uncle Eli. Ceil and Eli (who passed away in 2007) by then were in their mid 90's and as wonderful as ever. We all went out to dinner one night and Grandma Dorothy's name came up. Eli immediately started turning red and asked me if I remembered the "birthday" dinner from almost fifteen years earlier and then loudly exclaimed: "That woman! ... She always wanted something for nothing!" He was apparently not yet seeing the humor in all of this.

PART FOUR

Taking Care of Business

Chapter 17

The Center of the Universe

Living in Manhattan for thirteen years (before we moved to the suburbs in 2004) was an unbelievable experience for my wife and me and our kids. Everyone knows about the amazing restaurants and culture and the wonderful diversity in Manhattan, all of which we absolutely enjoyed. For me though, true Manhattan living also meant recognizing and understanding the strange quirks of living in the center of the universe.

Random Aside

While New York City technically (okay, more than technically) includes not only Manhattan, but also Brooklyn, The Bronx, Queens and Staten Island; most people living in the center of the universe consider New York City to actually refer only to Manhattan. I am not arguing this point, I am just saying.

If you live on the East Side you are much more likely to frequent East Side restaurants, shops and the like. The same goes for if you live uptown or downtown. This seems to makes sense, except that "Downtown" may be only a short walk, bus or cab ride away. Sometimes people who are simply hanging around on a Saturday, with really nothing at all to do, will feel better about what they "accomplished" if, for example, they live on the Upper East Side, and travel "all the way" to the West Side or Downtown. If they went to The Gap or Starbucks around the corner from their apartment they would not have much to report to their friends or co-workers when asked what they did last weekend. But, if they had been on a bus for ten minutes and traveled Downtown or to the West Side — perhaps to a Gap or Starbucks there or perhaps simply rode the bus across town and then back home — then their answer would be that they "went Downtown" or to the "West Side." Now they have "done something?" Of course, this is simply indicating a direction traveled and does not say much about what, if any, activities actually occurred (not really much different than saying "you drove five miles south on I-95"), but usually people are satisfied with the directional answer and do not ask the follow-up questions that would reveal that their friend or co-worker actually did nothing last weekend.

New Yorkers often rush even when they have nowhere to go. Sometimes I rush to get somewhere even when I am early so that I can try to squeeze in another task before my appointment or simply so that I would have more time to relax and do nothing. Now, maybe it is just me, but whenever I race across the street against the light and narrowly escape death from a speeding garbage truck, I uncontrollably smirk and make a whistle-like sound — something like "doo dadood doo doo!"

Whether in a rush or not, the subway is often the best way to get around Manhattan, but much like an elevator, it can be a very awkward place — people are packed so closely during rush hour that I swear they are unwittingly sharing all manner of DNA. There are no captive audiences any more "captive" than subway riders, and this can be annoying. I always hate when street performers enter a subway car and force everyone to listen to the same three bars of some song that they repeat each morning. The nice thing about street performers — performing in "the street" or at the park is that people can stop (if they have time and are interested) to listen, tip the performers if they feel entertained or just feel bad for them or they can move on and get away from the music if they think it's crap. It really is a perfect marketplace, where talent equals crowds and success. Then there is the off-key subway duet that you cannot get away from — their screeching noises and your inability to escape makes you feel like you are getting a cavity drilled or perhaps makes you even long for the dentist's chair.

Worse yet are the loud interruptions on the subway for the "excuse me everybody ...," bogus speeches by panhandlers and con artists of all stripes. I really find the rap of the teenage boys selling candy particularly annoying. If they simply explained that they are selling candy as a part-time job, the candy is fresh and tastes great and is a good value at $1.00, I would have no problem with them and would probably even buy some candy. But they say something to the effect of, "We are not selling for a basketball team or for the Cub Scouts, but rather to keep us off the streets and out of trouble." Implicit in the speech is that if they did not sell this candy and, more specifically, if you don't buy their candy, they will be forced (actually you cheap bastards will be the ones forcing them) into a life of crime — whatever. ("Whatever" is another word like "hello" that depending on the inflection has somehow taken on a totally different meaning, from the "whatever you want to eat" to the "Whatever!" that means "go #%&* yourself!")

Sometimes the heat during a summer in Manhattan, as it comes off the pavement and with the wind obstructed by tall buildings, is so bad that the exhaust from a passing bus can be downright refreshing ... almost as refreshing as the cool mist from a homeless man sneezing in your face. The first sign of a truly refreshing and street cleansing rain in Manhattan initially creates a stinky steam as the rain hits the hot, dirty and urine laden pavement, and then among the steam appear an army of umbrella salesmen. You can hear them in a singsong manner saying, "umm-brella, umm-brella, umm-brella!" on almost every corner of midtown Manhattan — usually right in front of a Starbucks. Where do these people come from? Perhaps they are the same guys selling knock-off bags and watches that scoop up their stuff in huge sheets with the first sign of cops? But where do they keep all the bags and watches when it rains and where do they keep all of the umbrellas when it is sunny? These are the questions that keep me up at night.

Random Aside

Also, what is with those strange sleeves that cover umbrellas? Once taken off, these "Umbrella Condoms" are difficult to put back on after the umbrella has been fully engaged and then is no longer in use — much like the experience with condoms, themselves. Might they be designed to prevent umbrella transmitted diseases or "UTDs," like when your unprotected umbrella is allowed to mingle with strange umbrellas in an umbrella stand at a restaurant?

Which brings me to a strange riddle: What do taxicabs, cops, condoms and pens have in common?

When you need a cab, a cop, a condom or a pen you can never find just one — you'll either find more of them than you can count on one hand or none at all.

A few times a year my wife and I go to a Broadway show and what is really annoying is the overused standing ovation. I have been to some shows that were average, at best, yet a busload of tourists who last saw the show as performed by middle schoolers in their small town, stand up and are in a standing 'O frenzy. Slowly, other tourists (and then even many New Yorkers) — feeling the incredible pull from the standing ovation peer pressure — begin to stand and add to the insanity. People start standing and mouthing "yup, yup, ... yup" like John Candy in the movie "Stripes" in response to: "Okay, who cried when Old Yeller died?" Then there are the stubborn few (I fall in this category) who refuse to get up if a standing ovation is not warranted — and remain seated usually arms crossed and eyes rolling.

I have also witnessed the opposite phenomenon at Yankee stadium — I am a lifelong fan and a season ticket holder. I was at a World Series game, the Yankees were in the field, there was two outs, two strikes and, of course, everyone stood up and began the rhythmic clapping rooting for the strike out and some rookie sitting behind me (who I am sure is the guy who started the standing ovation at the crappy Broadway show) is asking people to please sit down because he can't see. Of course, a few New Yorkers in my section — who were probably interested in making this tourist feel at home by helping him with the "rules of the road," barked that "it's the World Series ... and perhaps you should STAND UP!"

If you are only visiting New York then you might not know that on Halloween it can be difficult to distinguish between a person dressed up for the holiday and those that always look that way. It is the one day of the year that certain freaks blend in and look "normal."

Random Aside

Remember when people first started using earpieces for their cell phones and, before you realized they were on the phone, you thought the guy gesticulating and talking to himself was a crazy person? Years later, I now notice the opposite phenomenon. I see people walking alone in Manhattan who seem to be having animated conversations and assume that they are on their cell phones. Yet, many times as I get closer I realize that they are not using an earpiece or a cell phone for that matter. Instead, these happen to be actual crazy people that are blending in with the earpiece cell phone users. Who knew that the invention of the cell phone earpiece would have the unintended consequence of allowing crazy people to better blend in among the masses. I'm not sure if this is a good thing. In fact, I am pretty sure this is not good.

Invariably on Halloween, when I am spending many hours in an adult "non-Halloween" work setting, I forget what day it is. Then I go to a deli to grab lunch and wonder, for a moment, why the woman behind the counter is dressed like a French maid. After a few moments, I remember that it is Halloween and usually start daydreaming of all of the candy that I will soon eat.

I was in a diner one Halloween and noticed an elderly woman at the next table with a black eye patch. There was no other evidence (of a costume) to suggest that she didn't actually have an eye problem. And, even in New York, I thought it odd to find an 80 year-old (female) pirate. I could not help but feel bad that people would be approaching her all day saying things like "aargh" and "hey matey!" I think if I ever have a medical reason to wear an eye patch, I will just stay home on Halloween.

One of the great things about the city is that (because of its true "melting pot" quality) you can go out to eat and enjoy almost any type of food imaginable served authentically by folks that are often utilizing recipes that have been brought back from their homeland. There are locations where, within a few blocks of each other you could find good restaurants serving Italian, Indian, Thai, Chinese, Japanese, Kosher or French, among others.

Random Aside

Upon entering a new Japanese restaurant and seeing many Asian diners, I have heard people comment that the place "must be good" or something to that effect. While this may or may not be politically correct (I'm not sure anymore) these people are apparently comforted by seeing folks that, they figure, "must know this stuff"— to them I guess the restaurant was given a type of "Asian Seal of Approval." This makes me wonder whether Asians or Europeans are drawn to crappy American fast food restaurants, thinking that they must serve up good American fare because so many Americans eat at these places?

You can also get any type of food delivered to your door within twenty minutes. There was a Chinese restaurant that we would order from that delivered so fast, that we had to make sure we were actually ready to sit down and eat before calling. I would swear they were preparing the food on the way to my apartment — with a wok and hot plate rigged up to their bicycles.

Some of the delivery guys seem to have a death wish — they fly through the streets at night on bicycles usually traveling the wrong way down the street and dressed in dark clothing. I am amazed that five or six delivery guys are not killed each night on the Upper East Side. By the way, in case you were wondering why there are so many Chinese Restaurants in Manhattan, it is not because there are so many Chinese people, but rather because of the high concentration of Jewish people — we love the stuff!

Random Aside

If you live in a city populated by more than ten Jewish people, then not only should your city have a Chinese restaurant, but you should also understand that "Shapiro" is a Jewish last name — as Jewish as Schwartz, Rabinowitz or Goldbergsteinawitz. Yet, over the years some confused people have actually asked if I was Italian because "Shapiro" ends in a vowel? Then there are the "Shapiro's" (pronounced "Shuh-peer-row") or "Levine's" (pronounced "Luh-veen") who try to come off as WASP's by insisting that their names are pronounced "Shuh-pie-row" or "Luh-vine."

All the Manhattan food choices can make selecting what to have a difficult chore, particularly if there is a group trying to make this decision together. The "what do you want to have tonight?" question can lead to an interesting (if not annoying) debate on the merits of different establishments and types of food. Someone usually says something like, "Whatever you want, you choose ... but not Japanese because I had it last night." Then another might suggest Chinese, and the person says, "Oh that is so heavy, but really whatever you want." So then someone else might suggest a new Thai place, to which the person who was leaving the choosing up to everyone else usually says, "I hear that place is not very good." This person is then asked, what they want and, of course, they say, "Whatever you decide, I am up for anything!"

"I am up for anything," is definitely annoying to hear from the person who is really not up for much and is keeping hungry people from a good meal, but it does describe the great New York, New York. This city welcomes everyone from every corner of the globe and is a place where nothing is too big or too unusual. After living in Manhattan for some time, there is truly nothing one can see that should be too surprising — be it a man walking down the street with an iguana on his head, a cross-dresser on roller skates or someone in a chicken suit. I have seen them all. Every day truly is a new and unique adventure in the center of the universe — if you simply take note of the funnier details as they pass you by.

Chapter 18

Recommended Daily Allowance

In an effort to avoid my first heart attack, I read nutrition information labels and watch what I eat. Sometimes a twelve ounce soft drink and small bag of chips are considered to be more than one serving — as if a friend and I are likely to share this snack. The Tic-Tac markets itself as the "1½ calorie breath mint," although each one is about the size of a grain of rice. A piece of cheesecake that size is probably not much more than 1½ calories. Thankfully, though, they don't claim that a Tic Tac is suitable for sharing.

Many diners (either the food establishments or people that eat there) subscribe to the "cottage cheese diet" — as if cottage cheese is somehow the anti-fat/calorie. Apparently, all you need to do is add a scoop of cottage cheese to anything and it becomes the "health conscious choice." Bacon cheeseburger with fries and a scoop of cottage cheese — sounds healthy to me! Folks will also add a *diet* soda to this meal and feel they are really trying to be good.

Random Aside

Have you ever experienced the hotel mini-bar confession? You are out of town on business, you arrive back at your hotel room late after a dinner with clients, you have a pretty decent buzz and the mini-bar seems like such a great idea — so you eat a candy bar or two and some roasted nuts and wash it down with some soft drinks. The next morning, your buzz has worn off as you head to check out of the hotel. Of course you have done your best to completely put the mini-bar transgression out of your mind ... that is until you are settling your hotel bill.

The hotel clerk says with a condescending tone (and I'm sure she is looking at your, or rather my, gut) — "Did you have anything from the mini-bar last night?" It is like what I am sure going to confession is like ... "Sorry father, for I have sinned ... I had a soda and some roasted nuts," "Is that all (as she peers over her glasses)?" "Well, there was that Snickers bar and ... um the Milky Way bar too."

When checking into hotels, I always love the question, "Would you like the mini-bar key?" My reaction is always, "Are you kidding!?" Does anyone ever decline the mini-bar key? There is always really good stuff in there and usually when you need to hit it — and hard — you are not in a particularly picky mood. Hmm... maybe that is why people (and I should) turn it down?

Whole grain foods have always been considered (by actual health professionals) to be healthy, but as more and more people turn to these healthy options they demand more and more of a good thing. Multigrain bread? Sounds good, but just how many grains are we talking about here? Six or seven grain bread ... what a joke, our society now has 12 grain bread! Truth be told, I'm not sure what qualifies as a "countable" grain in this multigrain race for more of a good thing, nor do I even know how to tell whether what is being sold as a 9 grain, is really only (God forbid) an 8 grain. Do different sized sesame seeds get multi-counted? Yet, despite the "amazing" advancements in multigrainology, I still feel we, the human race, can and must do, and demand, better! We must strive for, and dream of, the day when we are able to reach the 20 grain level. Now that would truly deserve to be called a *multigrain* food product.

Once in a while I cook, although it usually involves grilling something on the barbeque. Ever notice how recipes you receive from family members are often rather inexact. A cup or teaspoon of an ingredient I can understand, but often the directions call for far less scientific measurements, such as a splash (how much is that?) or a dash (which I think is less than a splash, but I'm not sure why I think so) and an even smaller amount, although equal in terms of measurement precision — the pinch. Oh, there is one other, which I believe I first heard from my father, who referred to an amount of a particular ingredient he used as a "suggestion" — as in a suggestion of dill. What a "suggestion" means, I believe, is that you *think* about adding the ingredient, and actually take the top of the bottle off and wave the ingredient near the bowl, without actually adding any. Some of these recipes also direct that the dish be placed, not in the oven at 350 degrees, but rather in a "350 degree oven," as opposed to your other "400 degree oven."

Speaking of food quantities, many people shop at stores where they can get food in BULK — like the 20 gallon drum of Skippy peanut butter or the 30 lb. feed bag of Cocoa Puffs. Whenever I go to these stores, I see some of the largest people I have ever seen in my life. It always makes me wonder if they were skinny before they started buying in bulk or whether they have always been that size and these stores are simply more convenient places to stock up on their daily requirements?

Random Aside

This is really a modern day chicken or egg question or a nature/nurture mystery — much like I have wondered if some of the many strange lawyers I have met over the years became lawyers because they are strange or have become strange from many years in the profession? If you are not a lawyer, you may be saying to yourself now, "Talk about 'strange', look in the mirror buddy!" Truth is that some of my closest friends are strange lawyers, yet they concede that they are far stranger than I.

Many shoppers at these bulk stores seem to simply assume that if the item is sold in bulk it must be a bargain — like the large bottle of 400 vitamins. Often, however, the fine print on the bottle indicates that, for example, this is not quite the "one-a-day vitamin" that probably costs the same amount for 200 tablets, because you are supposed to take four of these vitamins at a time. One needs to understand this new or "fuzzy" math to shop at those stores, like when trying to figure out whether the 30 pack of paper towel or toilet paper is a bargain when the rolls are 36% skinnier, but 12% more absorbent, than the 24 pack you usually purchase at a higher price. So bring your calculator or abacus. And the bulk stuff expires, just like stuff sold in regular sizes — a fact seemingly overlooked by the bulk happy. So, buying a ten year supply of a product may not be such a great *idea*, even if it is a great deal ... unless it is Twinkies for your bomb shelter.

One of the things that people seem to love is the free food sampling at some of these places. Let's face it, people love free stuff. And people *really* love free food. In fact, one could argue that consumers love free food more than anything else given away, especially when you consider the meager value of the food given away, and just how excited consumers are to sample anything at anytime, like extra spicy Swedish meatballs at 7:00 A.M. And people come back for a second and third free taste, as they pretend to be considering the merits of the food item as if they were sampling a fine wine — "very nice finish ... kind of nutty" — well it is peanut butter, after all.

The end of any trip to the grocery store, bulk or standard size, involves the dreaded checkout line and choosing the same "wisely." There are people who make a living as professional "handicappers" — basically gambling market analysts — providing gamblers with advice on the wisdom of betting on a particular horse in an upcoming race or on a particular football team on Sunday. I have always thought these professionals could help when I am trying to decide which line at the grocery store is most likely to move the fastest and allow me to get the hell out of there, particularly important given that, by the time I hit the checkout, I usually have already been driven crazy by the 12-15 minute wait at the deli counter. This is more difficult than picking the Kentucky Derby Winner.

Random Aside

There was always a teacher (as far back as Middle School) who had a "vocal twitch" of sorts, repeatedly saying "uh" or "um." My friends and I would track and calculate "UPH's" or "Ums Per Hour" and place wagers on what the UPH rate might be for a given class period or bet the "over" or "under" relative to the "line" (the estimated UPH). Similarly, there was always a ridiculous guy in every law school class that felt the need to repeatedly raise his hand for the sole purpose of trying to demonstrate that he was really smart — which he often disproved on his own. One such guy ended up in a law firm I used to work at and at every department luncheon or seminar (for perhaps eighty people) he would insist, usually to no avail, on trying to prove how smart he was and how dumb everyone else was. This became insufferable and would lead to "over/under" bets with colleagues concerning how many utterances Mr. Smarty Pants would make and to disputes, such as how to measure a loud guffaw — which I always thought should count as half of an utterance.

Now, when picking which checkout line will likely move the quickest there are many, many variables to consider. The obvious considerations are the length of the checkout lines, the number of groceries the shoppers on line each have, the number of different types of groceries the shoppers have (aka grocery diversity), including those that might need the dreaded "Price Check."

More advanced analysis includes such things as the relative experience or inexperience of the cashiers, whether anyone on line looks like they might be a check user, and whether the register tape appears to be running low and might need to be changed before you are through. Invariably, despite careful and deliberate analysis, I choose the wrong checkout line: The skilled cashier goes on break and is replaced by a pimple-faced trainee, a guy in a jogging outfit inexplicably pulls a checkbook out of his sneaker, then the full register tape gets messed-up and the trainee needs a price check. Then, in an attempt to restore order, the sixteen year-old assistant manager is called in. This is the kid who just started shaving and is wearing a clip-on tie, a short sleeve dress shirt, jeans and black sneakers (apparently the promotion from stock boy to assistant manager requires an upgrade from white sneakers to the more business/corporate look).

While all of this madness is happening, and my blood starts to boil, there is always a fifty-sixty year-old woman with big hair and too much make-up in front of me who is desperately trying to make eye contact with someone, anyone. She rolls her eyes, as her hands move from her hips to up in the air and then back again in disgust. I look down at the floor, trying my best to dodge her glances. She wants desperately to (over)share her rage with someone else — usually, unfortunately, me (I must have that kind of face, despite my best efforts *not* to have that kind of face) — and say something like: "Did you ever!?" And in response to my blank stare she'll likely say: "Well, I never!"

Random Aside

By the way, I think it is simply bad form for checkout clerks to comment on one's purchasing decisions. I know some are just being friendly when they make harmless comments like: "Looks like someone is baking a cake." But, it gets annoying. As I am in the dairy aisle and loading, for example, yogurt after yogurt — of a type that my family was blowing through at one point — I begin to wonder at what point ... is it 10, 15, or 20 of this one item that will push the clerk to make the comment, "Wow, someone really likes ...!" I don't know why the thought of such a comment sends chills down my back, but it does. Perhaps because I have issues? Wouldn't a bright line rule here be good? No mention of what a customer places on the checkout conveyor belt? How about if the clerk said, "Wow, looks like someone has a drinking problem," upon scanning many cases of beer or "looks like someone has genital warts" or "a yeast infection," when ringing up the appropriate ointment?

After a few trips to the bulk food warehouse or after the holidays, people tend to gain a few extra pounds. What is interesting is some of the poor clothing decisions many people tend to make in an effort to mask the problem. Now it would seem that the general rule is pretty simple: The heavier you are, the less skin you should expose and the looser the clothing. Somehow this rule does not seem to be religiously followed.

A common mistake, particularly prevalent in the 1980s but still seen way too often, is when heavy people try to hide weight by squeezing into spandex or some other very strong flexible fabric. This is not the way to make yourself attractive. Now because sometimes tough love is appropriate, I will share a (quite nasty) saying that a friend of mine used in high school, which describes this "squeezed in" look: "Ten pounds of shit in a five pound bag." Think about that image the next time you try to squeeze 200 lbs. into a three inch by three inch garment.

In recent years the bare midriff has been a popular fashion trend, which is a good thing ... for some people. See, some do not understand that this is only a fashion trend; it should not be treated like a new county ordinance requiring everyone to show their belly. Showing off your belly is an option, assuming you don't have a "belly."

When you put on weight, there is the risk of developing an additional chin(s). If you get heavy enough, then apart from gaining a chin or two, you will actually lose the part of your body formally known as your neck. You know, that part of the body that your head is supposed to rest on — pedestal-like — and that is supposed to connect your head to your torso. If you stray too far from your diet, then what was once a neck becomes a mass of flesh that starts at or near the chin(s) and flows directly into the chest cavity, making it difficult to discern where one part starts and the other ends. Seeing a very large gentleman on my train has taught me something else, as well: Apparently a short-cropped beard that ends just beneath the first (i.e., the original) chin can be employed to give the appearance of a defined "start" to the neck. Perhaps the right type of chest hair configuration can similarly define the end of the neck and start of the torso?

When I was a teenager I could eat non-stop and I still had trouble putting on weight. This unfortunately changed in my adult years and, like many others, I now need to watch what I eat and be sure to exercise enough or else I start to develop that second chin and my pants start to ride a bit higher. Invariably I go through a stretch of time where I am less active and eat too much (and of the wrong things) so, I put on weight until I get back on track. A few years ago I lost some weight and people would ask, "How did you do it?" Is it really that complicated? If I eat less, choose healthier food options and exercise more, then I will lose the weight that I gained. Too many people simply lie to themselves about how "good" they have been because they add cottage cheese or a fad diet to their otherwise unhealthy routine. Of course, this won't take the weight off any more than the weight gain will be masked by a creative outfit or beard.

Chapter 19

Everything I Ever Needed to Know, I Learned at a Part-Time Job

I had a wide range of part-time jobs as a teenager and throughout college. Some of these jobs taught me skills that come in handy as an adult, while others simply provide interesting memories. My brother and I mowed lawns during the summers and shoveled driveways in winter, I worked at a deli, as a telemarketing cold-caller, valet parked cars and worked in bars doing everything from security, bar backing (guy who fills ice bins, re-stocks beer bottles and replaces kegs) and bartending.

Random Aside

One of the strangest part-time jobs I ever had, only for about a week when I was about twelve, was weighing and packing nuts in small plastic bags in the garage of an odd couple in my neighborhood who sold nuts at the Roosevelt Field Flea Market on weekends. I only lasted about a week as

> *it was so painfully boring being cooped up alone in this dark and dingy garage and because the guy's wife creeped me out. She was probably in her mid-60s, always seemed to be in a house coat and had this really weird way of speaking about her husband "Gene's" or as she would say "Geenaahaah's" nuts.*

I learned some valuable lessons during the summer that I was hired to make calls for a telemarketing company. "Let me assure you Sir, I am not trying to sell you anything...." And we actually weren't. We were trying to get these people to answer surveys, usually about consumer products and whether they had seen a particular commercial or bought or enjoyed a particular product, etc. We learned quickly that people, for example, in the New York area, were not likely to have the time or be willing to spend the time answering our questions. The amazing thing was that some folks — usually older and in less populated areas — were willing to answer surveys that took as much as forty minutes to complete! They would say things like, "It will take forty minutes ... oh, well, alright, let me just get my lemonade from the porch and settle in my comfortable chair...." This was, of course, the 1980s, with no Internet and much less television and far fewer infomercials to watch.

Confirming my own experiences, I will not give any cold-caller (for any reason) any of my time. I just won't. Even with the do-not-call lists, I still get the occasional call — from businesses or their "partners" that we have dealt with in the past. Some of these telephone solicitors will start talking really fast, without taking a breath — thinking that if they don't pause most (civilized people) will not interrupt them and will listen (and be enticed) by their spiel. Perhaps it was being hung up on so many times when I was doing the calling, but I am never deterred by their rapid speech pattern and simply interrupt them to say I am not interested. The caller will then often pause briefly — to find the appropriate response from their call sheet — and as I am saying "good bye" will again begin talking rapidly, as I hang up.

How about the cold-caller that says, as you answer the phone: "Please hold for Mr. Johnson." Doesn't that make you think: "Wow, Mr. Johnson must be so important ... he has an underling making calls for him! I shall now wait on hold (indefinitely) for this great and powerful man and buy whatever he is selling!"

One memorable sales call happened a few years ago, when a woman called asking for my wife. The dead giveaway that it was a sales call — this is before Caller Id — was that, with an accent that was definitely not "from around here" the caller completely mangled our last name, asking for Jill "Shaprio" or "Shapirino" or something. I then, in turn, asked what the call was in reference to?

Random Aside

As everyone should know, part of being a good spouse or a good friend or a good human, is that if you are the one that happens to answer one of these sales calls you get rid of the person — you "take one for the team." You don't suggest that they call back at another time or a specific time when the person they are looking for will be available, like during dinner or give out a cell or work number.

When I was working at a large law firm, I received a cold call from an insurance salesman. He initiated the call by telling me that he was speaking with another lawyer at my firm and that this "colleague," who he named, apparently thought that I might be interested in this particular insurance product. I

> *thought, and still do, that this was unbelievable. My "colleague" was not a close friend goofing on me, which would have been understandable. When I confronted this guy, who was not a friend, he sheepishly explained that he was having trouble getting the insurance salesman off the phone and "felt bad" that he wasn't buying anything. The "hold" that this insurance salesman had on him was apparently rather strong. It was like he was being tortured behind enemy lines and eventually (read: within five minutes), "broke" and was permitted to get off the phone if he agreed to give up a colleague's name.*

As for the salesperson calling for my wife, after she mentioned something about a "wonderful offer" I explained that my wife was not interested. Then the frustrated female solicitor, got all — for lack of a better way to describe it — "feminist" on me. She angrily barked: "Do you make *all* of the decisions for your wife!" Of course, this woman did not know that I am a caring sensitive man, who believes in equality for all and that I just might know my wife a little better than she did, including knowing that my wife definitely did not want to speak with her, let alone buy whatever crap she was offering.

I was a little surprised by the caller's rudeness and erroneous suggestion that I was a male chauvinist pig. Yet, instead of correcting her and being insulted, I thought it would be more fun and effective (in terms of pissing her off more) to instead feign agreement with her false accusations. I responded: "Yes, I make all of my wife's decisions for her ... and she cannot speak now because she is in the kitchen, where she belongs, making me dinner.

Goodbye." Of course, nothing could be further from the truth, but I am sure that this sufficiently pissed her off.

It is bad enough to listen to a long sales rap live, but how about the recorded sales messages. Who in their right mind would listen to a recorded solicitation? Let me get this straight, I should listen to a company's recorded sales pitch because they don't have the time to speak to me directly. I think they should have the common decency to allow me to hang up on a live person or, at least, to place a live person on hold for many minutes, just as companies always do to me when I call for "customer service."

While being a former telemarketer has not made me a hero at home, on many occasions my daughter (when she was about six) enthusiastically remarked how lucky she was that her dad was a former deli employee because I could make a good sandwich. When she would ask what I did as an Attorney, I would scratch my head and try to explain something to the effect that "I try to help companies run their business or with their business problems or in disputes with other businesses...." This was usually met with a glazed over look and an attitude that suggested that it was too bad I no longer did something useful, like sandwich making.

When I was a young boy, I told people that I wanted to be either a fireman or a lawyer (like my dad) and when asked what a lawyer did, I said, "They go to the City and bring home gum." That pretty much summed up (from my perspective) what my dad did. Everyone claims to hate lawyers — and many people really do and often for good reason, until they really need one. Truth is though, being able to make a good drink (from my bartending days) or sandwich (from my days working in a deli) comes in handy as an adult and certainly makes you more popular at certain social gatherings than being a lawyer. Also, the ability to drive in reverse well from a summer of valet parking, can be quite helpful.

Chapter 20

"Your Call is Very Important to Us"

A company that I used to work for years ago had a "help desk" that you were supposed to call if you had a computer problem. After ten-twenty minutes on hold they would almost always instruct me to "turn off my computer and then turn it on again." I always thought this was a modern day equivalent to kicking the side of your television to get better (pre-cable) reception. These calls also remind me of Mike Myers in SNL's famous *Coffee Talk* sketches: "Let me give you a topic …. 'The Help Desk' … it is neither a 'desk,' nor does it provide 'help' … discuss."

In more recent times a call to nearly any large company's customer service line, is met with a recorded message imploring me to listen carefully to all of the options as they have "recently changed!" It seems that every company's customer service phone options have recently changed — they are a moving target. Also, they always say that the call may be recorded for quality assurance and, most importantly, that my call is "very important to them." Of course, when was the last time you put a really important call on hold for twenty minutes? Would you do this to your boss or to someone that you were hoping to date?

Random Aside

I have had some terrible experiences calling large companies and dealing with their complicated phone options, extended holding times and their "customer service representatives." (This too could be a "topic" suggested by Mike Myers on Coffee Talk: "'Customer Service Representatives' ... they neither represent the customer, nor do they provide service ... discuss.")

Some movies tell "true stories" (the way this book does), while others are "based on a true story" — which I think means only minor details are changed and some editorial license is taken. Finally, there are the films that tell stories (like those told in recorded customer service messages) that are "inspired by actual events," which, in the movie context, could mean that there was, for example, once a guy named "Bill" who was a dentist, but everything else in the film is fabricated.

I never believe that my call is really important to these companies, nor that they recently changed their options or that their call volume is particularly high. Instead, it certainly seems that the importance of my call to these companies is directly related to the likelihood that I am calling to purchase something, rather than make a return or seeking technical assistance. My likelihood of purchase seems directly related to the "call volume" and my wait time or at least to how many people they pay to man the phones.

In fact, if it were possible to hear the internal monologue of the person recording the company phone options, I think it would sound something like this — be sure to listen to all of the options, as they have recently changed:

- If you want to place a new order, in other words, give us more of your money, then please press "1" and a very helpful (live) person will be right with you to take your credit card information and try to up-sell additional products that you don't want or need.
- If you have already given us your money, and don't intend to give us any more of your money today, and are seeking a refund or to cancel an existing order, then please press "2," but be warned that call volumes are very, very high for this type of non-revenue generating call and you should be prepared to wait a long time. Of course, if you don't want to hold, feel free to hang up now or at your next earliest convenience. Either way, remember that your call is very important to us!
- If you have technical questions and are under contract and/or under warranty, and again we have no hope of getting any more of your money today, please press "3," and wait for Ida — she is our least helpful representative who will be with you as soon as she finishes her third coffee break of the morning and gets to the fifteen calls ahead of you. Because our call volume is very high for these types of calls

particularly when you consider that we only have Ida handling these calls, please expect very long wait times. As always, if you would prefer not to hold, you have the option of hanging up and trying again some other time. Also, remember that another way for you *not* to speak to a live person is for you to go to our company website, where you won't have to wait on hold, but won't have your technical questions answered either.

- If your contract is expiring or you are no longer under warranty and want to spend more money on our quick and efficient technical support, then please press "4" and a member of our dedicated army of technicians will be right with you. Please have your credit card available and be prepared to pay through the nose for this support.
- If you still want to speak with a customer service representative, and you don't own a credit card or have any intention of spending any money today, please continue to hold for the next available representative. Her name is Mary Alice and she will answer your call eventually.
- If you press "0" in an attempt to speak with a (live) person, this call will be terminated because, if you had been listening to our recently changed options, like we had asked, then you would know that pressing "0" is not one of the options.

- Whatever option you ultimately decide to choose, don't forget how important, at least some of your calls are to us, and thank you again for calling the company that puts its (ready to pay now) customers first and the others on hold.

PART FIVE

Take a Good Final Look at Yourself and the Entertaining World Around You

Chapter 21

Have You Seen That Guy? Are You That Guy?

You don't need to be a face painter to be the guy with a weird look on his face or to be the guy doing something strange. These people are everywhere — sometimes they are just like you and me and sometimes they are you and me. Perhaps you or someone you know has seen or been, for example, the guy making the "mirror face" or the face many men make when looking in the mirror before a big night out or an important business meeting. You know this face — it is part primp and part bad ass.

Or just as likely you have been known to make the "wallet face." This is the face men make when, for example, removing their wallet from their pants pocket while sitting in the backseat of a taxi cab. From the look on this guy's face, you would think the wallet was being extracted from his butt.

Speaking of guys with weird looks on their faces, I think Keith Richards of the Rolling Stones should stop touring (even though I love the band) and allow himself to be carefully studied by the world's top scientists. Hear me out on this idea. They have done research on individuals who have had HIV for years and years, but never contracted AIDS, to see if there is something unique about their immune system or DNA that might help find a cure for this deadly disease. Well, as best I can tell, Keith Richards has been polluting his body for decades — drinking and smoking and who knows what else — yet the band plays on. We need to study this medical marvel — he may hold the secrets to many important medical breakthroughs.

Random Aside

If you are from my generation, then you might remember the excited look of the kid in your middle school class that got a chance to manually turn the film strip to the next slide? Of course, he would have to wait patiently for the loud "Beep" that meant it was "go time!" The film strip was like the technological equivalent of the early video game "Pong." I am tempted to make fun of the guys in school that were on the Audio Visual Squad and their facial expressions when they would attempt to service some of the technology, such as it was, but those early experiences with the film strip projector are probably what got people like Bill Gates started. So, I guess they were pretty smart and cool!

Surely you have seen the guy who willingly risks third degree burns in his mouth because he cannot wait for his food to cool. These are often intelligent adults who will eat blazing hot pizza (or cookies) knowing full-well that they may burn off their tongues, but simply cannot wait another minute for the thing to cool. They eat and try to put out the fire in their mouth at the same time by breathing in and out as they chew and make a sound like "huuh-a-huuh." Some of these people also feel the need to "test" just how hot their plate really is when warned by a waiter about a hot plate and they also need to see for themselves if the "paint is [still] wet" or whether the sign has been up since yesterday.

Perhaps you have experimented with the Pain/Release Phenomenon, but have not even known that you were doing so? Ever cut your fingernail a little too short? It leaves you with a dull constant pain. If you squeeze where it hurts it will, for a moment, hurt even more than it did before, but (here's the payoff) there is a moment just after the increased pain, when it will not hurt at all! Think "ouch! ... ahh! .. ouch! ... ahh!" This phenomenon occurs also after burning your tongue on pizza. When you scrape the burnt part of your tongue with your teeth it will hurt even more, but then for an instant there will be no pain at all. If you have not yet experienced this phenomenon, go ahead and try it, you will thank me.

A burnt tongue or just a tough day at the office can cause many to seek out stress relieving activities. Fun with the office paper shredder can be just what the doctor ordered here. I am not talking about shredding documents to keep them from the Feds, but just random paper that should be recycled, anyway. Come on admit how much fun it is to feed that paper to the shredder. For you (okay, maybe I am now just talking about myself again) it is like being a kid again and feeding some kind of hungry paper monster. Hey what do kids love better than destroying stuff anyway? Yet, this activity can be justified because it is a very responsible thing to do — ensuring that this paper gets recycled and once shredded the paper collects neatly in a bucket that can then be emptied into the recycle bin. Oh, the joy!

Although, once relaxed by the paper shredder or by simply leaving the office, it is usually not long before something or someone will prove to be downright annoying. For example, how about the guy at say a Spanish restaurant, that doesn't speak Spanish, but insists on interjecting a single Spanish word so that he can really develop a good rapport with the waiter: "Excuse me Sir, may I please have some bread and a glass of 'agua!'" Perhaps he adds in a "por favor" to sound truly bi-lingual. Or how about the guy who over-pronounces a foreign word, perhaps the name of an ethnic dish: "I will have the field greens, with the dressing on the side, and an order of your 'manaahgooot.'" See if you only speak English, you shouldn't say the foreign word as if English is your second language. Capisce?

Random Aside

Speaking of English as a second language, I had a young Russian barber — from one of the "Stans" — who always had a great joke for me, though sometimes there was a "lost in translation" issue. One of his jokes included a guy who had a particular male problem. "He couldn't ... eh, you know, 'pick it up,'" my barber explained. I looked confused until his hand gestures explained what he was talking about. Of course, I was thinking if the guy truly can't "pick it up," then he has a different kind of problem, which may be the envy of some.

There is an exception to this rule. When I was in Japan a few years ago and staying at the Westin Hotel, none of the cab drivers understood when we said "Westin" — they looked at us like we had three heads, even if they otherwise understood some English. We learned that the only way we could be understood, was to speak English slowly and then pronounce just the name of our hotel (with a Japanese accent), like this: "West-ah-Ween." That was the only thing that worked. This reminds me of the story I heard from a friend who was sitting next to a Japanese couple on an airplane who was approached by an impatient English-speaking flight attendant, trying to take their dinner order. The couple was asked very quickly "woud cha like chickin' or fish fa dinna ... chickin' or fish, chickin' or fish." The couple was startled and confused, so my friend turned to them and said, slowly, "for dinner ... Chicken or Fish?" The couple responded and were very thankful for the assistance. The flight attendant then asked my friend "if he spoke Japanese." While he does, he explained to her that he was, in fact, just speaking English, slowly and clearly!

If you are encountering annoying restaurant patrons (over-pronouncing foreign words or whatever) at a restaurant that you frequent, then you are also liable to encounter the really annoying guy that always thinks you go to that restaurant more often than he does, simply because he seems to run into you every time he is there. These people say things like "hey Jim, do you *live* here or something?" Yet, each time they see Jim at that place, aren't they there too?

Random Aside

Have you ever noticed that most people trying to meet up in a crowded public place pick the same place to meet as everyone else trying to meet up with someone at that same crowded place. Examples of this include the information booth at Grand Central Station or "The Bat" at the old Yankee Stadium. "How am I going to find you among over 50,000 people?" "I know, we will meet at The Bat and try to find each other among the 25,000 people trying to find each other."

Truth is we are all, to some degree, creatures of habit. When you commute to and from work everyday, this phenomenon seems to become more pronounced. Not long after I moved out of Manhattan in late 2004 and began life as a commuter, I began noticing that many commuters, myself included, took the exact same train every morning and many nights, and perhaps do this for forty years until they retire or die, whichever comes first. Once in a while I am the guy whose routine is "totally thrown off" and I catch a train in the morning that leaves ten or fifteen minutes later. What a way to start a day! With so many things in life requiring thought and careful deliberation, I suppose we develop routines that allow us to run on auto-pilot and save our brain power for more pressing concerns.

If you have ever rushed to get to the train station or to an appointment, then you also probably took part in the "traffic confession." I know I have. This is when a driver accidentally cuts someone off, who is then steaming mad and positioning to run them off the road. The only way for these drivers who have sinned to make things right is for them to give the look and gesture, which says, "I'm the idiot ... I am guilty of being the worst driver on the planet, and I am sorry for being born." (Think: hand in the air and sheepishly shaking head, while mouthing "Sorry"). This usually calms down road rage guy slightly, mainly because the repentance has confused him, and he often lets the drivers off with screams of, "That's right you are an idiot!"

Have you ever been the guy with all manner of stuff tied to the roof of his car? This too can lead to road rage incidents, particularly if the roof-rack payload is not properly secured. I certainly have been this guy too; most memorably in the early 1990s during a trip I took to Syracuse with my friend Michael Ditkoff (aka "Ditty") to help him relocate for his last two years of medical school.

Random Aside

A friend named Pete helped move me into my college dorm in the summer of 1987 — well, he didn't really provide any "help" in the normal sense of that word, but he (and I) did have a great time for the few days that he visited. Actually, Pete had a much better time than I did during my first few days of college. I certainly had fun and met many people, but was also busy during the day buying books, registering for classes, getting my dorm room set up, etc. Pete, on the other hand, had nothing but time on his hands and seemed to meet and party with nearly every person (by day and night) in my quad. During the following week, one person after the other who had been introduced to me by Pete came by looking for my friend. Of course, I explained to them that Pete didn't go to the school.

"You're funny!," or, "Good one!" they would say. Eventually, they learned that I really wasn't trying to be funny ... at least not that time.

Well, Ditty needed a bed for his new apartment; so off we went, two straight guys, shopping together for a new bed at a Syracuse-area department store. I recall lying down on a bed to test it out and patting the bed while suggesting that "honey" come try it out. (As the saying goes: "Not that there would've been anything wrong with" Ditty and I being a couple, but in Upstate New York in the early 1990s, this didn't seem to be so well-accepted, and making the salesperson uncomfortable was good fun.).

Anyway, the beds were really expensive so we decided to keep looking and stumbled upon a great store that manufactured and sold mattresses and box springs right on their premises. This was all they did at this place and the quality of their product and their prices were fantastic. Ditty and I were congratulating each other on our fine work, as the store's very helpful staff secured the mattress and box spring to the roof of Ditty's car. The "tie-down" was not accomplished with rope, like I would have expected, but rather with a plastic strap-type material. I started to wonder if this was the best idea, but then thought better than to question these "experts." After all, what the heck did I know about this business? This store only sold mattresses and box springs and presumably all day, every day, they were asked to tie these things to the roofs of their customers' cars.

Ditty and I were driving with the new purchase down a secondary road at about 40 miles per hour and everything seemed great until our roof cargo first started to wobble ... and then flap up and down wildly. An instant later we heard loud noises like "PHEEEW," "PHEEEW," "PHEEEW," as the plastic straps snapped and came undone. As if in slow motion, Ditty and I watched through the rear view mirror of his car as the mattress and box spring flew and spun high in the air. Cars behind us screeched loudly to a halt to the left and right of these large items that scattered in the road. Ditty quickly pulled over about 100 yards ahead of his (now newish) mattress and about 110 yards ahead of his (now slightly distressed) box spring.

Amazingly, no car accidents resulted, but traffic was now obstructed. My initial relief that no one was killed was followed by anger as I noticed a man running into the road and grabbing hold of Ditty's mattress. "Hey, what the ...," I started to yell, while sprinting toward Ditty's purchases, until I realized that this guy was not a mattress thief, but rather a Good Samaritan pulling the items to the side of the road to protect the public safety. Oops! After we thanked this nice man and dusted him off from my take-down (just kidding, I realized my mistake just before trying to tackle him), Ditty went to find some rope and I vowed to never again be the guy with stuff improperly tied to the roof of his car!

Chapter 22

Life is Full of Material

They say that whatever doesn't kill you will make you stronger — or just really sick — or something to that effect. I have also come to realize that although I would often like to kill (in a metaphysical sense) a real jerk or obnoxious person, it would be best just to enjoy the humor in their behavior. Believe me this is still a self-actualization work in progress, but over the years I have tried to remind myself that many people have serious "issues." Of course, as has probably become obvious to you, I have issues too, but I am talking about anti-social and offensive issues.

Jerks and critically obnoxious people are all around us — people who think that they are the only ones on this planet or the only ones that matter or are just plain mean or nasty. High school or college age kids are often not shy about getting right in the face of these people and telling them just how much of a jerk they are, along with many other choice words. I know I was never shy about doing this. Then I suppose I truly became an adult (or maybe it was when I became a parent), when I began to realize that these people have significant issues that should, in a weird way, be celebrated.

It seems that really obnoxious behavior often expresses itself at the airport, when people are under the stress, real or imagined, of traveling. One weekday morning years ago I was on a very long security screening line for the Delta Shuttle. I was probably the twentieth person on a forty person single file line that was moving very slowly. I had a heavy bag with documents needed for my day-long business trip that I rested on the ground in front of me and every two to three minutes, when the line moved up a few feet, I would move it forward.

While waiting in line I realized that I needed to check for something in my bag, so I bent down to check inside it for a moment. While I was doing this the line budged forward — I was now the nineteenth person on line and still a good forty feet (and probably twenty minutes) from the security screeners — but for an instant there was a two foot gap between me and the person on line in front of me. "We have a situation here!" It was perhaps ten to fifteen seconds into this "line gap situation," when I located what I needed in my bag and was starting to inch forward. Just then, however, the guy on line behind me, without saying a word, picked up his bags, and stepped out of line and in front of me — squeezing into the two foot gap that I had recklessly left unprotected for a moment.

Puzzled by this strange behavior, I think I said something like, "Excuse me, Sir?" He then said, with a southern accent and plenty of attitude: "Hey buddy, if you're gonna mess around back there, then you lose your spot on line!" My "messing around" lasted about fifteen seconds, but more importantly, this guy just moved up one spot and was now the proud owner of the nineteenth spot on line! Wow, with these types of maneuvers just think of all the time he must save in his travels, not to mention all the friends he must make along the way!

Random Aside

It may come as a surprise to some that this jerk was not a New Yorker, but that would be a misnomer. First of all, New Yorkers are much more courteous than many people think, as they have become accustomed to long lines and crowds and pulling together with their fellow man during much more trying times than a long line at the airport. Also, it is my belief that New Yorkers have learned, generally, to deal with run of the mill inconveniences and only get loud and obnoxious when the circumstances are really outrageous. More importantly, however, most New Yorkers are savvy enough to understand that if they pull this kind of crap with the wrong guy (think Tony Soprano or one of his friends), he will take their head off.

Anyway, I had an epiphany, of sorts, at this moment. Instead of getting really mad and escalating the situation like I would often have done in the past, I realized that, although I am far from perfect and have some (okay, many) unresolved issues myself, I would not like to be *this* guy who has some serious, serious issues. I just started laughing and saying to myself, (but loud enough that he could hear) "Wow, that is classic" and then, still laughing I mentioned a few times as the line inched up "wow, you really saved some time" and "you are almost there now!"

If this had been a movie scene, I would have surreptitiously slipped metal paper clips in the cuffs of the guy's pants and perhaps in his pockets. He would then have been delayed as the screeners tried to determine what kept setting off the metal detectors. The guy would then get loud and hostile with security because he was running late (and because he was a jerk) and would end up being arrested and taken "in the back room" for a more thorough (read: "cavity") search. Unfortunately, the real scene did not play out that way. I do think the guy was almost embarrassed by my shaming, but I'm sure he would do it again, so be sure not to "mess around" next time you are in line at the airport.

Rather than always letting a jerk like this get me upset, I *try* to think of their existence as a good source of comedy. Perhaps they will even provide material for a book someday? What guys like this don't realize is that, thankfully, most of the time most "crisis situations" in life, are not real crisis situations — they are not about life and death — but we, nevertheless, overact as if they were.

The thing is that everyday and every aspect of life is chock full of "gold" — of material that can be enjoyed and laughed about for years to come. We must, however — at least sometimes and even if only for a few minutes — not take ourselves or the pressures of everyday living too seriously. This does not mean shirking responsibilities at work or at home, but rather when things seem like they cannot get worse and then they do, trying to see the humor in it all. When someone on a bus, at the office or on the street does the most bizarre thing imaginable, think of it as free comedy. I suppose it is all a matter of putting life's pressures and the oddities of everyday living in perspective. Also, I think it is critical that we force ourselves to look at our surroundings a little differently and, of course, enjoy a good laugh.

Chapter 23

Extra "Free" "Bonus" Stuff

In some of Burt Reynold's movies of the late 1970s and early 1980s, they included outtakes or "bloopers" during the credits. This was the first time I can remember seeing this type of material, although I don't know if those movies started this phenomenon. Whatever the origin, ultimately a market was created for outtakes and mistakes. On television you could find shows about television bloopers, shows about home video mishaps, and ones about animals attacking or about car chases and wrecks. Over time, particularly with the introduction of DVD's, outtakes and mistakes seemed to morph into "deleted scenes" and, more generally, "extras." Everyone loves the "value" of something "extra" — like the new and improved household product that provides 20% more "free" stuff than the cheaper box you purchased last week.

Movie scenes and material are filmed today, with little or no intention of ever being included in the theatrical release, but rather simply to create some of these "extras." Don't get me wrong, I like a good "extra" as much as the next guy and, thus, it seemed only appropriate to add some "extra," "free," "bonus," stuff here.

Rejected Alternative Book Titles:

Taking Care of Business ... in the Men's Room

Am I the Only One That Notices This Stuff?

Is It Just Me?

Is It Just Me ... or Are You Also This Twisted?

Strange Observations of the Basically "Normal"

Rejected Advisory Care Instructions:

Our litigious society has spawned disclaimers in ads and on products, some that border on the ridiculous. The radio disclaimers that are read so quickly that no human could possibly understand them don't seem to make much sense, nor do the disclaimers in microprint that speed past the television screen. Also, how about the medications that warn both that the product may cause drowsiness and may prevent one from falling asleep?

Books, like this one, perhaps should contain disclaimers to make clear that, while it is intended to be entertaining, there are no guarantees that it will induce laughter, let alone a belly laugh, while also warning that reading the book does significantly increase the risk of experiencing excessive laughing and perhaps even pants wetting, particularly if the reader has a bladder control problem.

Similarly, many products include specific instructions regarding proper use and care. Below are some of the rejected (or "extra") advisory care instructions for this book:

For best results, lighten up and stop taking yourself so seriously.

Store in The Can after opening.

If ingested, induce vomiting.

Keep out of reach of small children and the very tightly wound.

Edges of paper can cause paper cuts.

Flammable, if placed too close to fire or other heat source.

Machine washable, tumble dry low, remove promptly and hang.

Rejected Testimonials:

Testimonials in newspaper movie ads are enjoyable when there is a huge disparity in font size between the favorable quote and the less than famous source, like this:

"THE GREATEST MOVIE EVER!"

Bert Mandelbaum, Short Hills Mall Coupon Circular Insert

Here are some of the rejected testimonials for this book:

"DON'T HIT THE MEN'S ROOM WITHOUT IT!"

Sam Jones, Janitor Weekly

"BETTER THAN A ROOT CANAL."

(Some jerk that didn't like the book)

"IT BURNS WELL."

(Jerk's friend)

"THE BEST BOOK I EVER READ!"

Mom

About the Author

Jonathan S. Shapiro has a unique perspective on human behavior and interaction, as well as life's funnier details, because of his innate analytical nature and his eclectic background. As an elementary school child, Shapiro often got into trouble with neighbors and teachers on Long Island when he would offer them his honest assessments (borne out of his critical analysis), whether solicited or not, and point out when they were dead wrong on a particular point.

He later honed and demonstrated his analytical skills as a *Phi Beta Kappa* student at S.U.N.Y. Stony Brook, where he devoured sociology and psychology courses; at Fordham Law School, where he graduated Cum Laude and was an editor on the *Fordham Law Review*; as a successful New York attorney, first with the international firm Weil, Gotshal & Manges LLP and then as a partner in his own midtown Manhattan law firm; as an adjunct professor at Fordham Law School; and as a published author of numerous scholarly works.

Shapiro currently lives in Westchester County, New York, with his wife and their two children. Of course, the fact that Shapiro is married, a father of two and is a Jewish lawyer who grew up on Long Island is not unusual. The fact that he is all of those things and is also a former standout high school football and lacrosse player, as well as a former deli employee, valet parking attendant, telemarketing cold-caller, bartender and club bouncer is much more unusual.

Shapiro has interacted with every walk of life over the years. He has always looked at the world a little differently and has utilized his photographic memory to record his unusual observations in *Shapiro's World*, including how to find humor in the otherwise insufferable people and situations that we are all forced to deal with on a daily basis.